A SQUARE SKY
A True Story of a Prisoner In Afghanistan

Ahmad Sharifi
Dorothy Keddington

Copyright 2002 by Dorothy Keddington & Ahmad Sharifi

ISBN: 1-930980-72-8

All Rights Reserved.

No portion of this book may be copied or duplicated by any means except by written permission from the publisher. Inquiries should be directed to:

GRANITE PUBLISHING AND DISTRIBUTION
868 North 1430 West
Orem, Utah 84057

Library of Congress # 2002102664

Printed in the United States of America
First Edition, 1995
Second Edition, February 1996
Third Edition, March 2002

Cover Design: Tammie Ingram & Steve Gray
Map: Ahmad Sharifi & Michael Keddington

ALSO BY DOROTHY M. KEDDINGTON:
Jayhawk
Return to Red Castle
Shadow Song
Flower of the Winds
The Mermaid's Purse

and the soon to be released
new novel Aisling of Eire

Authors' Note:

In preparing and presenting this book, every effort has been made to ensure accuracy and authenticity. In a few cases, some names have been changed, or partial names have been given, to protect those still living. It should be noted that several variations exist in the spelling of certain Afghan names and words. In such cases, the authors have chosen one of the commonly accepted spellings for such words and names.

It should be noted also that the secret security organization instituted during Taraki's regime was initially known as A.G.S.A. The name changed to K.A.M. under Amin and finally became Khad under Karmal. For the sake of simplicity and consistency, the authors have referred to this organization as Khad throughout the book.

To My Father

Introduction

HARI RODE IS the name of a beautiful river that runs along the border of Afghanistan and Iran. If only that river could speak! It would tell thousands of stories about hundreds of thousands of people leaving their homes and families in the search for freedom. Freedom that was taken away by the shameful Russian invasion of Afghanistan. Yes, if only that river could speak. Every drop of it, full of the people's tears and prayers, would whisper the tragic verses of their sad destiny. Out of all those verses, one is about to take the shape of a song called "A Square Sky...."

Sayed Ahmad Sharifi

Chapter I

Kabul, Afghanistan - August 1979

LAUGHTER, WARM AS the sun-baked walls, filled the pleasant room where twenty-six-year old Sayed Ahmad Sharifi sat cross-legged on the floor engaged in a lively game of *Kahrumboard* with three of his closest friends. Ahmad had arrived at Samad's house the evening before, along with Zia and Bismilah. Since Friday was the weekend in Afghanistan, the young men often took turns spending the night at each other's homes. After playing cards, chess and the billiards-like game of *Kahrumboard* for much of the night, they had slept in late and enjoyed a leisurely breakfast of tea, toast and eggs. Now they were at it again, competitors as well as friends, promising the losing team would buy fresh fruit for the others.

Sitting on Ahmad's left was Samad, with his green eyes and smiling, clean-shaven face. The two had been classmates throughout secondary school and college. Samad shared Ahmad's love of music and poetry and had played the *tablas* on the night of Ahmad's engagement party.

Then there was Zia, tall and shy, with lean cheeks that would redden at the slightest mention of girls. And Bismilah, always an emotional opponent, with his silly, drooping mustache and clever black eyes.

Of the four, Samad was the most European-looking, while Ahmad, even dressed as he was now in dark slacks and a button-down shirt, was strikingly Afghan. His hair and beard were jet black, and his eyes a tawny brown that sparkled with the glow of amber whenever he was excited. Yet, in his face there was nothing of the fierceness or cruelty that history and tradition attributed to his race. The first and only time Ahmad had held a weapon in his hands was the summer he visited a cousin who lived in the mountainous province of Nuristan.

The two teenagers had gone hunting one morning and Wakeel excitedly handed Ahmad his rifle as a game bird flew overhead. Ahmad aimed and pulled the trigger, then watched in sick horror as the wounded bird fell to the ground. Remorse compounded the sickness as he stared at the bloody result of his actions. Giving the rifle back to his cousin, Ahmad adamantly refused to go hunting again.

That same summer, another incident reinforced his aversion to killing and violence. Ahmad's Uncle Nazif had been traveling a rugged mountain trail with a friend when the men came upon a large Bengal tiger sunning itself on some rocks. Struck with the beauty of the magnificent animal, Nazif stood quietly still, watching the tiger. Before he realized what was happening, his companion raised his rifle, fired, and the tigress lay dead.

Nazif was so enraged by the senseless act, he gave his friend a sound beating and refused to accompany him any further. After the man had gone on his way, Nazif discovered two small cubs near the dead mother, and carried them home.

Ahmad and his cousin were given the task of feeding the cubs milk from baby bottles, and long after Wakeel had tired of the chore, Ahmad remained. Fascinated with the young tigers' every move, he would watch and play with them for hours.

Then, as now, life was Ahmad's passion, not games that ended in death.

Ahmad leaned forward to pick up a game piece, his dark eyes intent on the wooden board in front of him. For a moment, the room's only sound was the lazy whisper of the fans shushing the hot summer air. Then the quiet, as well as his concentration, was rattled by a demanding knock on the front door. Startled, Ahmad glanced out the window to the courtyard where Samad's little brother ran to answer the summons. Like most Afghans living in older sections of Kabul, Samad's family occupied an L-shaped dwelling built of dried brick. The living quarters were separated from the street by a large courtyard and high walls built of the same muddy brick. The courtyard not only afforded privacy for the family, it also provided space for a few trees, flowers and often, a small vegetable garden.

From his position near the open window, Ahmad had a clear view of the yard as well as the double doors in the outside wall. One of the doors stood open, yet he couldn't see anyone outside. This immediately struck him as strange, as most friends would enter an Afghan home without knocking.

Moments later the boy was on his way back to the house, calling, "Ahmad! Your brother's here."

Ahmad put on his shoes and sport coat, unable to shake the worrisome feeling that something was wrong. Crossing the courtyard, he stared at the half open door with a puzzled frown. His family and Samad's had known one another for years. If one of his brothers wanted to see him, why didn't he just come inside?

Ahmad reached the doorway and his worried thoughts froze into fear.

Waiting outside the walls was his older brother Hafiz, both wrists bound in steel handcuffs, and a look of mute apology in his eyes. Surrounding Hafiz were four well-dressed strangers, their *kalashnikov* machine guns a deadly contradiction to the civility of dark suits and ties.

"Don't move!"

"Turn around and don't do anything stupid!"

Ahmad stared at the machine guns aimed at his chest and his legs went weak. Shock, fear and a thousand questions flooded his mind, but his dry mouth was incapable of uttering a word.

"We don't want to frighten you," the tallest man informed him, while another grabbed his hands and snapped on a pair of handcuffs. "We just want to ask you some questions. But first, we need to go to your house."

Seizing his arms, two of the strangers dragged Ahmad toward a black Russian Volga which had been hidden from view by the high walls. After shoving him into the back seat, the two men climbed in on either side, while the others got in the front with Hafiz between them.

As the car drove away, Ahmad caught a final glimpse of his friends who had rushed outside to see what was happening. Fear had drained the life from their youthful faces.

All the laughter was gone.

* * *

Heat rose from the dusty roads and reflected off the baked walls of the ancient city as the Volga sped down one of Kabul's main streets. Through the din of traffic and busy market places, past mosques and modern hotels, the black limousine drove steadily on. Inside the car, the only sounds were the engine's soft hum and the dry scrape of matches as the men lit cigarettes. To Ahmad, it felt as if that small space were dominated by a ponderous, deadly silence. His eyes were focused on the familiar streets of Kabul, but his mind was racing, imagining all the horrible things that could happen to him and his family. Only the familiar sight of his older brother sitting in front of him, offered any comfort.

The tense, half-hour drive ended on a mountainous road in an area of the city known as Baghebala. Here, the two brothers were ordered out of the car and forced to walk at gunpoint up the long dirt lane leading to their home. As the silent procession made its way, neighbors left the coolness of their houses to see what was happening. Others stared with wondering, accusing eyes from their windows.

Along with the sun's glare, Ahmad felt the heat of shame and embarrassment. He had never been in any kind of trouble before, and to be paraded up the street like a common criminal added humiliation to his fears. Whenever his eyes chanced to meet those of a friend or neighbor, he quickly glanced down and tried to pretend he didn't see them.

Finally, they reached the high walls and front door of his father's home. Inside, a steep flight of stairs led the way to a large inner courtyard where flowers bloomed and fruit trees offered shade from the blazing Afghan sun.

Ahmad's family rushed out of the house to meet them, then huddled in fearful silence as the armed strangers shouted orders for no one to move.

Ahmad met the anxious eyes of his wife Zarghuna, who held their two-year-old son in her arms. Near her were his mother and stepmother, his sisters and younger brother Rahim. Fortunately, two older brothers were visiting with friends or Ahmad feared they might have been arrested as well. Only his father remained inside, but Ahmad could see the older man watching from the window of his room. Glancing up at his trembling form, Ahmad could feel the man's shame as if it were his own. This was ten times worse than the curious scrutiny of neighbors.

All his life, Ahmad had wanted nothing more than to make his father proud of him. His older brothers had often given their parents cause to worry, especially Zoor, whose tendency to get into fights had earned him somewhat of a reputation. Of all his brothers, Ahmad had been the only one to graduate from Istqlal, an exclusive French high school, then go on to college. Just four months ago, he had earned his degree from the University of Kabul. Ahmad's greatest reward had been the look of pride on his father's face. Not the shame he was seeing now.

What had he done? Why were they doing this to him?

"Which room is yours?" the tall stranger demanded.

Silently, Ahmad showed him the way, then waited in the hall, while three of the men searched and ravaged his possessions, and the other man stood guard.

Not only Ahmad's room -- the entire house was ransacked. Couches and chairs were broken. Mattresses ripped open. Books tossed from shelves. The strangers even looked under the rugs and on top of the roof. Ahmad was amazed when he saw them taking apart his stereo and rifling through the tapes. From their comments, he gathered they were searching for documents or proof of some kind. What documents could he possibly have which would be of interest to men like these?

The search went on through all sixteen rooms. At its end, Ahmad felt a wave of relief when the tallest of the four strangers, called Riza by the others, removed Hafiz' handcuffs.

Then Riza approached Ahmad. "We need to take you in for questioning," he said shortly. "Then we'll let you go."

Ahmad was shaking from the inside out, but managed to give the man a respectful nod before turning toward the door.

Sensing all was not right and that the well-dressed strangers were somehow to blame, little Jossef ran after his father. The two-year-old had always been precocious and quick to mimic the speech of others. Now he burst out with a familiar curse often heard from his uncles.

"God damn your father!" he cried, angry tears streaming down his round cheeks. "God damn your father!"

The harsh words sounded strange coming from the mouth of a child, yet poignantly courageous. Enduring the little boy's condemnation with silent disdain, the men allowed Ahmad to bend down and kiss his son. Then his sister Shaima hurried forward to pick up the crying child.

Tears stung Ahmad's eyes as the four men urged him away from the sunny courtyard. Glancing over his shoulder, his gaze swept over the faces of his family. The gentle, pain-filled eyes of his father ... his beautiful mother, Alima, and his father's first wife, whom the family called *madarak,* meaning dear mother ... his wife and dark-eyed sisters ... Rahim, the younger brother he adored ... Hafiz, his friend and teacher, as well as older brother ... and Jossef, his dear son.

Ahmad couldn't rid himself of the oppressive fear that this might be the last time he saw any of them, yet there was no time for words of farewell. In those brief, final moments, their eyes became their tongues, expressing all the love that could not be spoken.

Walking down the hill, shock and fear blinded Ahmad to the curious stares which followed him. When they reached the Volga, one of the men took a dark cloth from his suit pocket, bound it tightly around Ahmad's eyes and the sunlit afternoon went black.

Chapter 2

WITH MY EYES blindfolded, my other senses became more alive to everything around me ... the click of a cigarette lighter and smell of tobacco smoke ... the sound of the men's breathing and the soft rubbing of their clothes when they moved. Most of all, I could feel their ugly presence.

I was alone with four men that I found myself hating and fearing more than anyone. Where were we going and what did they want from me?

In recent months, I had heard stories of arrests and abductions. One night, as I was walking home from a movie, I had seen two members of the secret police chasing a young man through the streets. They finally cornered their victim in an alley, then filled his defenseless body with bullets from their machine guns.

Even so, it was difficult to believe this was happening to me. I took some deep breaths, trying to control the fear, but it didn't help.

After a while, the tightness of the blindfold began hurting my eyes. When I tried moving my eyebrows and cheeks to loosen it a little, one of the men slapped me hard on the back of the head.

"*Nakoh!* Stop that!" he ordered.

I straightened up, smarting from the blow, and remained still.

Even though I was blind, I could tell from the various turns the car made, which direction they were taking me. I was surprised when the Volga stopped a couple of blocks away from the school that I had attended for twelve years. Then I realized where we were. *Sedarat.* The Department of Justice and Office of the Ministry. The place had been built a long time ago, at least sixty or seventy years, and thick, high walls separated the huge complex of buildings from the rest of the city.

Over the hum of the engine, I heard a noise that sounded like steel doors opening. Then the Volga moved slowly forward. Seconds later, the driver braked and switched off the engine.

After dragging me out of the car, two of the men grabbed my arms and led me across what seemed to be a parking lot. My blind steps jerked to an awkward halt in response to those who held me, then a gruff voice ordered me to bend down.

By now, the blindfold was loose enough that when I leaned over, I had a glimpse of a small door directly in front of me. The next moment, someone kicked me hard from behind. With my hands cuffed behind me, there was no way to brace myself for the fall. I hit knees first and face down on a rough cement floor, and pain exploded through my body.

The next moment, strong arms yanked me to my feet. As the men dragged me across the floor, I was vaguely aware of the warm wetness of blood trickling from my right ear. Both of my knees were bleeding as well.

Then someone removed the blindfold.

Still dazed with pain, I stood squinting in the sunlight. My captors and I were in a large, dirty courtyard completely surrounded by high walls of muddy brick. Hurrying toward us was a short man with thinning brown hair, a thin mustache and narrow green eyes.

"You got him!" he said with satisfaction.

The one called Riza nodded. "Yes, sir."

"Where is your brother-in-law?" the green-eyed man demanded.

I answered in a choking voice. "I don't know."

"You don't know? Do you want to see him?" he asked with a sneer. "Look over in that corner."

I glanced in the direction he was pointing and discovered my sister Mina's husband standing near one of the high walls. Even from a distance of several yards, I could see that Farid had been badly beaten. His clothes were covered with blood, and he was hunched over in pain, both hands clutching his stomach. A soldier with a machine gun across his lap sat nearby.

The shock of seeing my brother-in-law in that condition silenced the throbbing voice of my own pain. Farid was a doctor, and a kind, generous man who would do anything for anyone. Many times, he had walked miles into the mountains to treat poor villagers, then refused payment for his services. Farid had helped members of my own family as well, and we all loved him. He and I had a double relationship, since I married his sister and he married mine.

Our eyes met across the dusty courtyard. The moment was brief, but long enough for me to know these men intended to kill him.

I glanced away and discovered the green-eyed man observing our wordless exchange with interest.

Nodding to the soldier who held me, he said, "Take him to the main office."

This was a small room with white-washed walls. A wooden desk, some filing cabinets, and a few chairs comprised the simple furnishings. The guard who had brought me removed my handcuffs, while the soldier sitting behind the desk shoved a small book in my direction and instructed me to sign my name. After doing so, I was taken across the hall to a much larger room.

"Wait here," the soldier said and shoved me inside.

If there is a hell in this world that we live in, that room was the perfect example. I felt as if I were living my worst nightmare; that what I was seeing couldn't be real ... hundreds of men moaning and crying, their clothes torn and bloody ... some lying on top of each other, a few moving about, others just standing with zombie-like stares. The entire room smelled like blood and vomit. There was blood on the walls, the floors, everything.

I stood in the doorway, shaking with shock, not wanting to believe what I was seeing ... the broken noses and hands, the missing teeth, and open wounds ....

"Go and sit down," the soldier ordered, then left me alone with my nightmare.

The nearest available space was next to a middle-aged man whose eyes were swollen and bleeding. The man's right eye was completely out of its socket and hung down against his cheek. I glanced away from the horrible sight, not knowing what to say or do.

An uncomfortable silence followed the soldier's departure, one in which I could feel the curious stares of everyone in the room. Since I was the only one who hadn't been tortured, it wasn't difficult to understand why. Some time later, I heard voices in the hall. The next moment, a soldier entered the room.

"Sayed Ahmad Sharifi!"

As I got to my feet, the soldier grabbed me by the arm and told me to come with him.

I was taken to another office, larger than the first, where several soldiers in khaki Russian-type uniforms were sitting at a long table. Two guards with machine guns stood on either side of the door. One of the soldiers got up from the table and handed me some typewritten forms.

"Answer all the questions," he said shortly.

I sat down with the papers on my knee and looked over the list ... *Where were you born? What is your father's name ... what school did you attend ... what languages do you speak* .... The questions went on and on. There must have been forty or more. I paused when I read: *Why were you brought in?* then wrote: *I don't know.*

When I had finished, I signed my name at the bottom of the last page. One of the soldiers took my right hand, put my thumb on an ink pad, then pressed it on the paper next to my signature. Another motioned to the guard who had brought me. Without a word of explanation, I was taken back to the same nightmare room I had waited in before.

The man with his eye hanging down made room for me on the floor beside him, then asked in a lowered voice, "Why did they bring you here?"

"I don't know. They told me they were going to ask me some questions, then let me go."

"They tell everybody that," he answered. "Let me give you some advice. No matter how much they torture you, don't give them what they want. They're going to kill us all anyway."

* * *

As the hours passed, I battled with my fears and tried to prepare myself for the worst. I told myself I wasn't any better than the men around me. If they went through it, so would I. But I wanted to get it over with. There's a saying in my country: *The fear of a monster is a bigger monster.* Whenever I heard the slightest noise in the hall, my eyes and ears were completely alert. My worst enemy was my own impatience, and of course, time. It seemed to me as if the hands on the clock were traveling around the globe with the speed of a turtle to add only one more minute.

During those long hours of waiting, I said every prayer that I knew. I called the names of every holy place and every holy man I had ever heard of and begged them to help me. Glancing out the room's single square window, I could see that it was beginning to get dark. By now, there were many other newcomers like myself, in addition to those men who had been tortured. Glancing around, I estimated there must have been two hundred or more men in that miserable room.

Eventually, two soldiers came to the door and ordered us to follow them. One soldier led the way, while the other brought up the end of the line. Those who hadn't been tortured tried to help the men who couldn't keep up, because the soldiers kicked and hit anyone who lagged behind. After crossing a high-walled courtyard, we were taken to a large room much like the one we had just left. Also like the first, there were a hundred or more tortured men inside, sadly awaiting their destiny.

Another hour of waiting and wondering passed, then the guards brought dinner. Most of the prisoners were too badly injured to eat and their food went untouched. So did mine, but for a different reason. Uncertainty and apprehension, along with the stench, had my stomach in knots.

During dinner, I found myself sitting beside two muscular young men. They asked my name and told me theirs -- Quassim and Ibrahim.

Quassim was easily six feet tall, with broad shoulders and an oriental cast to his features. His black and white striped shirt was open, revealing a gold chain which hung on his hairy chest. A deep cut marred one cheek and a narrow stream of blood trickled from his nose. As we talked, Quassim muttered an occasional complaint about his stomach, and turned his head to throw up.

When I expressed my concern, he just shrugged and said, "It doesn't matter."

Like Quassim, Ibrahim was also tall and broad-shouldered, but his hair and trim mustache were a light brown. He, too, showed the effects of recent torture. His once-white shirt looked more like a bloody rag, the holes exposing numerous cuts on his chest and arms.

Looking into his brown eyes, I sensed a gentleness in Ibrahim that wasn't present in his friend. Something about his soft-spoken voice and polite manner put me at ease and made me feel I could trust him.

Both men wanted to know why I was here, and all I could tell them was, "I really don't know. I think it has something to do with my brother-in-law."

Not long after dinner, we heard the harsh shouts of a soldier outside in the yard, calling out various prisoners' names. I watched with growing anxiety as the men whose names had been called, got to their feet and silently left the room.

Ibrahim and Quassim explained that there were two torture shifts -- one which went from seven or eight at night until five or six the next morning; and the day shift, which ran from seven a.m. until six in the evening. Those prisoners who had been tortured that day or the night before were usually given a day or two to recover before their names were called again.

I rubbed my sweating palms against my slacks, wondering if and when I would hear my own name called.

As evening deepened into night, a soldier came to the door every few hours to ask if anyone wanted to go to the bathroom. During one of these calls, I joined the group of prisoners on their way outside to the latrine. We were walking across an open, muddy courtyard when I heard someone call my name. Glancing to my right, I saw my brother-in-law in a small room with bars on the window.

"What did I have?" he asked in a heart-wrenching voice.

I immediately understood what Farid wanted to know, as he and Mina were expecting their first child any time. Hoping for the chance to speak with him, I hung back near the end of the line.

"I don't know -- " was all I could say before a soldier kicked me, and I went down on my face in the mud. After that, I didn't dare make another attempt.

When I got back to the room with the other prisoners, Ibrahim made space for me to lie down between him and Quassim. I was grateful for his kindness, but there was no way I could sleep. Not with the screams and cries of those being tortured echoing through the walls of nearby rooms.

Seeing the fear in my eyes, Ibrahim offered a few words of comfort. "It's not so bad. Don't worry. You'll get used to it."

Used to what? I was afraid to ask, although I desperately wanted to know.

"How long have you been here?" I inquired instead.

"Since yesterday," Quassim told me. "Ibrahim and I work for the radio station. We were arrested there."

As we talked, both men offered the same advice I had been given earlier. "No matter what they do to you, don't tell them anything. Don't put anybody else through this...."

I nodded soberly, remembering the frightened faces of my family when the strangers had searched and terrorized our home.

After a while, Ibrahim fell asleep and Quassim and I talked quietly together. We talked about our lives and our families far into the night, until he, too, drifted off to sleep.

A single bulb cast its sallow light on the tortured bodies huddled around the room. A few men were fortunate enough to have a thin blanket or dirty gray sheet between them and the cement floor. Most were not.

I wrapped my arms around my knees, struggling to control my fears. During the daytime, the sunlight had given me a small feeling of security, but now, everything seemed more horrifying. The sights. The smells. And the sounds. Even the smallest noise seemed magnified. Every time I heard the actual sound of the beatings and the pleas of the unfortunates, I would close my eyes and imagine myself being in their place.

My imagination was growing wilder every moment and I needed to focus my mind on something other than the hell I was in. From the room's small window, I looked out at the night sky. It was full of stars, but there was something different about it. The window and huge walls of the prison made it look square. I had never seen the sky like that before. The more I looked, the more it made me think. Inside that square sky I found myself reliving my past. I saw my present. I could even imagine my future. It was as if the square sky knew all the secrets of my life and was testing the capabilities of my mind and body, by playing with my weaknesses and emotions. Out of all those feelings, fear was too strong to overcome, and passion for life was too sweet to let go.

All night long, I ran wildly through the darkest mountains of my emotions, searching for the soothing arms of my family and friends. The square sky painted their smiling faces and the blinking stars echoed their loving voices, but wouldn't allow me to squeeze them tight into my thirsty arms. Instead, I was drowning in the haven of memories and imagination.

At last I saw the sun's rays chasing the brightness of the stars that were about to cover their eyes with the golden blanket of the dawn. With their final fading glance, I felt as if those starry eyes were promising me they would return soon, to take me once again to the land of escape and the fantasy world of freedom and reunion.

I had shut my eyes for a few minutes of exhausted sleep, when I grew conscious of footsteps in the hall outside our room. The sound got louder and closer. Through half-shut eyes I saw a soldier and four important-looking men in dark suits and ties enter the room. Two of the men were Afghan and I was fairly certain the other two were Russian.

Taking a rigid stance in front of them, the soldier pointed at me and said, "That's him!"

Chapter 3

AT THE SOUND of the soldier's words, the blood rushed to my head and a sick weakness turned my stomach. I'd thought I was prepared for this moment, but now that it had come, fear and dread made me so light-headed I could hardly stand. Putting a hand down to keep my balance, I got to my feet, conscious of the cold sweat trickling from my forehead to my eyebrows and nose.

"Turn around and put your hands behind your back!"

I did as the soldier ordered and felt the bite of steel hand-cuffs close around my wrists.

Not another word was said as we left the room and headed down a long hallway. The four men in suits led the way. I followed behind, with a soldier on either side holding my arms.

I was sure they were going to kill me. Why else would these important-looking men have come here so early in the morning?

It must have taken nearly ten minutes to reach our destination and those minutes were both the longest and the shortest of my life. As we walked down the halls and through a large courtyard to another area of the prison, I felt as if my mind were traveling thousands of miles per hour, frantically recalling the pale and petrified faces of my family after my arrest, the laughter of my friends and the memories of my beautiful childhood. The images passed through my mind faster and faster. Out of that spinning kaleidescope, two images stood out with painful clarity -- the innocent, tear-filled eyes of my father and the angry face of my son when he was swearing at the men who arrested me. With every step, Jossef's words echoed over and over in my brain .... *God damn your father ... God damn your father .....*

    Tears filled my eyes. Even though I blinked them back, my throat ached with the need to cry. The more I tried to hold back the tears, the harder it became to breathe, until soon, I was choking. Desperate for breath, I lowered my head and awkwardly lifted the lapel of my sport coat with my chin. With my mouth against the fabric, the choking sobs came out sounding more like coughs.

    Our destination turned out to be the same office where I had filled out forms the day before. One of the men crossed the room to open a door which led to another, much larger room. Here, I saw a wooden table, some chairs and a few filing cabinets. Seemingly out of place was a metal bucket full of water which stood beside one of the chairs. Then my attention focused on three strange-looking machines -- metal boxes with hand cranks and long wires hooked to them -- which lay on the carpeted floor. A mixture of curiosity and dread washed over me as I stared at the machines, and my body began to tremble.

Still, no one spoke. The two Russians sat down, arms folded across their big chests. Leaning against the side of the table was a tall, heavy-set Afghan with a sullen expression. The Russians were not small men, but the Afghan towered over them all. If possible, the man's presence was even more intimidating than his size. Bushy black brows met in a slanting scowl over bulbous, heavy-lidded eyes. There was something in his eyes -- a gleam of barbaric cruelty that the elegance of his well-cut suit, gold watch, and polished shoes could not disguise.

In the interim, the two soldiers had positioned themselves on either side of the door. One of them told me to sit on the floor, which I did.

Moments passed in tense silence. Every now and then, the big Afghan would glance impatiently at his watch. When the flat of his hand returned to the table, his gold sleeve button tapped against the wooden surface. That small tapping seemed magnified a hundred times in the room's uneasy stillness.

I wondered why no one was talking. Was it out of respect for the big Afghan, or were they all thinking about something they didn't want me to know?

Suddenly, the door burst open and the green-eyed man who had questioned me about my brother-in-law rushed into the room. He was breathing hard, and his stringy hair was wind-blown and out of place, revealing a large bald spot on the top of his head.

The others in the room tried to hide their smiles and laughter, but he knew something was wrong with his hair.

"Oh, I hate the wind," he muttered, trying to comb the strands in place with his fingers.

The big man leaning against the table wasn't amused. Glancing at one of his associates, he gave a short nod.

I had the impression they must have done this sort of thing many times, because his co-worker immediately understood the signal.

The man rose from his chair and approached me. "Get up and take off your clothes!" he ordered.

I stared at him, feeling a hot flood of embarrassment. Ten strangers in the room, all of them watching me, and I was supposed to get undressed?

As I struggled to my feet, one of the soldiers left his post by the door to unlock my handcuffs. My fingers tingled as the blood flowed back into my hands, and I made the mistake of pausing to massage them.

"Take off your clothes!"

The order came again, this time even stronger, with an ugly emphasis on each syllable.

I took a deep breath and started to pray. When I was younger I always prayed, but it was just a routine part of my life that I never thought deeply about. This time it was different. Every word of that prayer, I meant from the bottom of my heart. I was sure that God was listening to me, that He was going to help me.

The next moment I felt a painful kick in my side. The blow was so strong, I fell to the floor, grabbing my injured side with both hands.

"Get up and do what I say!" the man shouted.

In painful humiliation I obeyed. When I stood before them, my shame and body naked before their eyes, the man ordered coldly, "Now sit down!"

Squatting beside me, he began wrapping the bare wires from the metal boxes around my fingers and toes. At the same time, one of the soldiers ordered me to lie down, then shoved his heavy army boot against my neck. Another soldier grabbed my trembling legs.

Suddenly, a sharp, burning pain was boiling my blood and my entire body started to shake. I had heard in many languages, the expression of seeing stars in the daylight. That's exactly what I was seeing. My eyes were blurry and my mind had a dark picture with a spark of light going on and off.

After what seemed like an eternity, they stopped cranking the machine.

"Where is Farid?" the green-eyed man demanded. "Where is your brother-in-law?"

I tried to answer, but my tongue kept getting in the way. The effects of the electricity made it feel like a big piece of dry wood inside my mouth.

One of the soldiers dipped a glass into the bucket, then tossed the water in my face.

Gasping, I licked my lips. "I don't know where he is," I said. "You showed him to me yesterday ... in the corner of the yard."

"Where would he go if he had to be free?"

Something in the way the question was phrased gave me a small spark of hope where Farid was concerned, but my answer to them was still the same.

"I don't know ...."

The soldier bent down and removed the electrical wires from my fingers and toes. This time, the wires were wrapped around my ears. When they started cranking the machine, I felt like my head was smoking. The pain was unbearable.

"What group do you belong to?"
"Where is Farid?"
"What group do you belong to?"
"Where is Farid?"

The same questions, asked over and over, filtered through the sound of my screams. The electrical torture stopped long enough for that blessed splash of water and the only answer I knew how to give -- "I don't know ...." Then it began again. Blinding pain. Lights flashing in my brain. And the voices, shouting questions again and again.

My answer and the torture remained the same for over ten hours. Only the faces changed. Occasionally, the Russians asked their Afghan counterparts a few questions, but most of the time, the two men sat in silence, observing my agony with their flat, expressionless faces and pale eyes.

If anything could be worse than the pain, it was the humiliation. Those bare wires were wrapped around every extremity of my body, robbing me of my dignity as well as my mind. I felt worse than an animal. There were times when I felt as if I were sitting on a fire and my torturers were making that fire burn higher and higher. I wished that it were a fire. At least then I would burn and die. This kind of torment went on and on.

As the hours passed, my mind became blind. There was only the pain and the fear.

* * *

Sometime late in the afternoon, I was taken from the torture room, across a large courtyard to another area of the prison. My legs were so weak and shaky, I couldn't walk on my own. Two soldiers dragged me between them, then threw me into a large room occupied by around fifty other prisoners.

I lay on the floor, teeth chattering, hugging my clothes to my shaking body. My mind was still too shocked from the effects of the electricity to function. All I could do was lie there in silent agony.

Eventually, I must have fallen asleep, because the next thing I knew, the heat of the day had passed and long shadows were stretching across the walls.

The man sitting next to me, whom I recognized as the one with his eye hanging down, put a gentle hand on my shoulder and told me it was time for dinner.

I shook my head, unable to stomach the thought of food.

Not long after the dinner hour, I heard a rough voice shouting my name. I glanced up and recognized the cruel face of one of the soldiers who had brought me back after my electrical torture.

"Get up and come with me," he said.

I could barely stand, let alone attempt an escape, but he still snapped a pair of handcuffs on my wrists before taking me to a small room where five men were waiting. This time they were all Afghans. The well-dressed Russians were gone.

As I stood in the doorway, a stocky man with dark eyes and a thick black mustache, swaggered over to me. "So this is the one who doesn't want to talk," he said, a half-smoked cigarette between his sneering lips. "We'll make him talk."

Grabbing me by the neck, he yanked me off my feet and shoved me against the wall. The man's viselike grip was so tight, I couldn't breathe.

"Open your mouth!" he snarled, then shoved his cigarette inside my mouth.

Choking and helplessly kicking my legs, I spit out the burning tobacco. The man burst out laughing and released his hold on my neck. Still laughing, he left the room.

I rubbed my bruised throat and glanced nervously at the four men remaining. Sitting at a table in one corner of the room was a fat Afghan with curly black hair and a wrinkled suit. He sent me a glowering look as he got up from the chair, then, with a lift of his brows, gave a wordless signal to the soldier who had brought me. The soldier stepped forward and freed my hands from the metal cuffs.

Then, once again I heard the humiliating command: "Take off your clothes!"

Seeing the man's heavy army boots, this time I didn't hesitate to obey. After I had undressed, the soldier grabbed my hands and cuffed them in front of me.

"Lie down on your belly!" the fat man barked out, giving me a hard kick in the back. The next moment I felt his foot on the side of my head, pinning me to the floor.

There were no electrical machines in the room, but in one corner I had noticed a large stack of sharp-thorned branches. My heart beat hard and fast as one of the soldiers tied my feet with a rope, and planted his booted foot on my ankles to hold me down.

Then a short, swarthy Afghan wearing a dark suit, got up from his chair to approach me. In one hand he carried a thick, whip-like cable made of sharp wire.

I looked at the cable and grit my teeth, trying to brace myself for the pain.

Beginning with the heels of my feet, the man started to beat me, working his way up my body and flailing away at my bare flesh as if I were nothing more than a piece of meat.

"Who are your friends?"
"Give us their addresses!"
"Which group do you belong to?"
"Why haven't you joined the Communist party?"
"Tell us the names of your friends!"

The beating was so painful, I started making up names and addresses that didn't exist, hoping it would stop. Instead, when one man grew tired, another took his place, as the same questions were asked again and again.

This went on for hours until my body was drenched in blood and the walls soaked with my screams. When their arms were too tired to wield the wire cable, they resorted to using the sharp-thorned branches. Finally, the four men formed a circle and started kicking me. They weren't even bothering to ask questions any more, just kicking me from one side of the room to the other like a soccer ball.

One of the blows sent me slamming head first into the wall and consciousness spun away into blackness.

Chapter 4

A SMALL, DARK-EYED boy walked along one of Kabul's dusty roads, kicking a round rock from side to side with practiced concentration. Nearly every morning in good weather, Ahmad enjoyed a solitary soccer game during the two-mile journey to his school. The game fascinated him. And when Ahmad was fascinated by something, he poured all his energy into it, both body and soul. It didn't matter that he didn't own a soccer ball. Not when there were plenty of rocks to be had. But selecting the right rock was important. It had to be round enough, just the right size, and without any rough edges which would scuff his shoes. Even so, his shoes inevitably ended up with a hole in the toe, and always in the same spot.

Once Ahmad arrived at school, he would carefully hide his rock in a safe place, then retrieve it when the school day was over for the journey home. If he had a hard day or was feeling angry, the rock bore the brunt of his frustration. And when he was happy, it rolled smoothly along the dusty road before him.

Growing up in the comfortable middle of a large family, Sayed Ahmad Sharifi never considered himself a favored child. When he was born on the last day of winter in 1953, Latif and Alima Sharifi had been hoping for a daughter. Ahmad's father already had two sons by his first wife and another by Ahmad's mother.

On March 20, instead of a daughter, a fourth son was added to the family.

As a baby, Ahmad was sickly and fretful, crying much of the time. Doctors were unable to diagnose the cause of his illness, but his mother never gave up hope that her little son would survive. Many a time, when Latif rose for his morning prayers, he found Alima slumped in weary sleep outside the door of their room with the baby over her shoulder. Then one morning when Ahmad was almost a year old, a black cat was found dead in his bed. Ahmad's parents didn't consider themselves overly superstitious, but it couldn't be argued that from that time on the child's crying stopped and he grew strong and healthy.

Ahmad was not yet two when the long-awaited daughter, Mina, was born. Sweet and good-natured, everyone loved her, Ahmad included. In the years following, four more daughters were added to the family, then a final son, giving Ahmad's father two wives and ten children to provide for.

Latif Sharifi was a man accustomed to hard work and the responsibility of providing for a family. The oldest of five children, he was only twelve when his father died. His mother had no formal skills, and was forced to go to work as a seamstress, often sewing day and night to provide for her children, the youngest an infant of only six months. Because of his mother's long hours at work, Latif assumed much of the responsibility for raising his younger brothers. After graduating from high school, he sought work wherever he could find it. His keen mind and clever hands were skilled in many areas -- everything from carpentry and painting to mathematics and building designs. Eventually, based on his natural ability and talent, Latif became an architect for the Afghan government without ever having earned a formal degree.

During Ahmad's childhood years, the Sharifis moved often, living in rental houses all over Kabul. Ahmad was fourteen when his father was finally able to buy some land from the government on a hilltop overlooking the city. Latif designed a home for his family and they all worked together to build it. Ten brothers and sisters working side by side, following the skillful instructions of their father in laying the hard clay bricks. To save money, the family moved in before the roof and doors were finished. This presented some difficulties for Ahmad's mother and stepmother, but to young Ahmad it was an adventure. Like many Afghans, he loved nothing better than sleeping outside with the night sky for his ceiling, under a brilliant canopy of stars.

Over the years, more rooms were added to accommodate the Sharifi's large family, as well as the Afghan's unique sense of hospitality which extended to other relatives, friends and total strangers. In the Sharifi home, all guests were friends of *Allah*.

Although they were never considered wealthy in terms of material goods, Ahmad's parents bestowed a different kind of wealth upon their children. The richness of example and love.

Ahmad adored his mother. He and the other children called her *Bibi,* meaning queen. Although he never really understood why his father had two wives, Ahmad accepted his stepmother's place in their life with respect and affection. Many times as a child, he could be found curled up on her lap, listening to her wonderful fairy tales and stories from long ago.

As regular as the sunrise, Ahmad's father rose early for his morning prayers. A gentle man who loved God, music and poetry from around the world, Latif was never happier than when his family was gathered around him.

His father's generosity and exacting sense of fairness made a lasting impression on young Ahmad. One example was the time Ahmad had been promised a new pair of shoes for school. The family was short of funds, and in order to buy groceries, let alone shoes, Latif decided to borrow some money from a friend who owned a business in downtown Kabul.

Ahmad and his father arrived at the man's office one afternoon only to find he wasn't there. Ahmad could see by his father's expressive face, how disappointed he was -- to bring his son all the way downtown for a pair of shoes and then not be able to keep his promise. On their way home, Ahmad's father met a business acquaintance who greeted him with pleasure and excitement. The man told Latif he'd been looking all over for him because he wanted to buy some blueprints and building plans that Latif had designed.

He handed Ahmad's father five thousand *afghanis* on the spot as downpayment for the job.

After the man had gone, Latif stared at the money in his hands. God truly worked in mysterious ways. Here, he had been going downtown to try and borrow money and then someone walked up and handed him five thousand *afghanis*.

Ahmad got his new shoes that day and more. On their way home, father and son passed through a marketplace where vendors were selling barbequed beef and lamb kabobs. The tantalizing smell was more than Ahmad's empty stomach could stand.

"Dad, I'm very hungry. Let's get something to eat," he pleaded.

His father readily agreed. "In fact," he added, "wouldn't it be wonderful if we got some kabobs for the whole family and took them home! Then we could all sit down and enjoy them together."

Ahmad didn't think it was wonderful at all. Especially when he had to endure the tempting smell of those kabobs all the way home. But as much as he disliked having to wait, that experience opened up new windows of understanding. Ahmad was suddenly aware how much his father loved their family; that his first thought was to share the benefits of his good fortune with everyone.

Latif's generosity was enjoyed not only by his own children, but members of the extended family as well. Every year, Ahmad and his brothers and sisters looked forward to the gifts and activities associated with the Moslem holiday of ID AL-FITR, the "festival of breaking the fast," much the same way Christian children anticipate receiving toys at Christmas. ID was a wonderful celebration, a time of forgiveness, and a special time to visit family and friends.

But there was one year that Ahmad didn't receive any gifts. Instead, his father bought groceries, clothes and toys-- even a new bicycle -- and took them to the children of Ahmad's widowed aunt.

Ahmad's initial reaction was the same as his brothers and sisters -- disappointment fueled by anger. He could still remember the way they had all yelled and complained to their father after finding out what he had done.

"What is this? You bought him a bicycle and we didn't get anything! What kind of father are you?"

Then came Latif's quiet response. "Okay, that's good. Tell me anything you want. At least you have a father you can say these things to. Your cousins don't have that any more."

At the time, Ahmad was too caught up in his childish anger to understand what his father was trying to tell them. But that soft answer remained in his memory for years to come, long after new clothes and toys would have been discarded and forgotten.

Latif had a way of building teaching moments into the architecture of his children's lives, moments that became subtle blueprints of wisdom and love.

On cold winter nights he would gather his family around the *sandaly* and read them poetry, stories or verses from the Holy Koran. Latif would sit cross-legged at the head of the *sandaly,* a low table some three feet by two feet, common to every Afghan home. Beneath the table, a small charcoal-filled stove warmed the surrounding area where mattresses, blankets and pillows were spread.

Wrapped snugly within the folds of a comforter, feeling the body heat of his brothers and sisters on either side, with the dignified figure of his father sitting before him, young Ahmad felt safe, secure and surrounded by love.

Latif frequently offered an added incentive to his children. Whoever stayed to listen the longest could earn an *afghani* or two. As hard as he tried to do otherwise, young Ahmad usually fell asleep and one of his older brothers would garner the prize. But the richness of the stories told and the beauty of language were forever his.

Ahmad's love of language and learning became evident soon after he started school. His grades were consistently at the top of his class and he was especially gifted in the French language.

In a country where illiteracy was as high as ninety per cent, Latif was determined that his children would have the advantage of attending Kabul's finest schools. Having some exposure to as well as a fondness for the French language, Latif enrolled all his sons in Istqlal, a French school with a reputation for scholastic excellence. As time passed, Ahmad's older brothers Habib, Hafiz and Zoor either transferred to other schools where the requirements weren't so strict or dropped out altogether. Ahmad not only stayed, he excelled. When he was in the seventh grade, his test scores earned him special advancement into a higher level French class.

Ahmad had an added incentive for earning good grades that year. Slender and blue-eyed, with long dark hair, Madame Manguie captured Ahmad's teenage heart the moment she walked into the classroom. His new teacher was not only pretty, but friendly and kind. Ahmad was smitten. He couldn't take his eyes off her. From the first day on, he couldn't wait to go to his French class. Soon, he was taking more time with his appearance, making sure his wavy black hair was neatly combed, washing his face and carefully ironing his clothes. Ahmad was always in his seat at the beginning of class, eagerly awaiting the teacher's appearance. He even found out Madame Manguie's schedule, so he could see her when she came out of another class. These "accidental" meetings often resulted in her pausing to say hello and talk with him. Ahmad's day was immediately made brighter by one of her warm smiles.

School had been in session for about two months when his bliss came to an abrupt end. Madame Manguie took Ahmad aside one day to inform him that he was being transferred out of her class. Ahmad was crushed and confused. When he asked why, Madame Manguie didn't have a ready answer. In fact, she herself didn't understand the reason for the change, but assured Ahmad she would talk to the school's Director and find out.

A few days later, Madame Manguie sought Ahmad out and tried to explain the reasons for the transfer. But how does one explain prejudice and politics to a thirteen-year-old boy?

The directors of the school, who were French, had placed Ahmad at a higher level because of his test scores and ability; their Afghan associates objected to someone of the Sharifi boy's "lowly station" being in the same class with members of the royal family and sons of government officials.

Ahmad listened with a sinking heart, as his teacher tactfully explained that he could no longer attend her class for "political reasons." What did politics have to do with learning a language? Or fairness, for that matter. Ahmad's one consolation was the fact that Madame Manguie seemed genuinely sorry about the change, and he resigned himself to 'worship from afar.'

Most of the young men in Ahmad's new class were too old to be attending school, so the administration put them all together in one large remedial class.

The teacher was a pleasant woman who, although she wasn't as pretty as Madame Manguie, possessed excellent skills and knowledge of the French language. One skill she lacked, however, was the ability to control and discipline her students. On test days, they cheated openly and during lessons they refused to listen.

Ahmad was frustrated with the situation, but far from beaten. Instead, he sat on the front row, plying his teacher with eager questions. It wasn't long before she recognized the spark for learning which burned in her new pupil. The more she taught him, the more he wanted to know. Especially where French grammar was concerned. There were even times when Ahmad's teacher didn't have the answers to his questions and had to do additional research to satisfy the young man's thirst for knowledge.

Throughout the years to come, Ahmad's skill in learning languages expanded to include Pashtu, Urdu and Farsi, but the romantic flavor of French never lost its sweetness on his tongue.

It was during high school that Ahmad and many of his fellow students got their first taste of Communism. Like the first sip of alcohol, it seemed harmless enough. Attractive little books had been passed out by some of the students, whom Ahmad later learned were trained Communists. He had read some of them. One was about a devoted mother whose son dies for the cause of Communism. Another told of a man who was working to move a mountain. When friends mocked his efforts, the man explained that he knew the mountain could not be moved in his lifetime, but he was beginning a great work that his grandson would someday finish.

Then there were the times Ahmad and other students had been urged to leave their regular classes for lectures in Marxist doctrine. They had gone, glad for the excuse to get out of class, more than any real interest in what was being said.

For the most part, what was said made sense. The speakers talked about people's problems and mistakes the government had made. They told Ahmad and his friends there was a way to change things.

To the people of a country frustrated with poverty and centuries of sameness, Communism seemed to offer the bright promise of hope. In those days, it was certainly nothing to be feared.

Ahmad was aware that some of his high school friends were Communists. Zalmay Karmal, for example. He and Ahmad played on the same soccer team and Ahmad had visited his home several times. Zalmay's older brother Babrak was actively involved in the *Parcham* faction of the People's Democratic Party of Afghanistan, and reputed to have important ties with Moscow. Whether this was true or not, Ahmad had no idea, but Zalmay was a popular young man and played good soccer.

The *Khalqi* wing of the same party was led by another Communist, Nur Mohammad Taraki. Nearly everyone in Kabul knew about Taraki's frequent bouts of drunkenness and few had respect for the man. Ahmad saw Taraki's adopted son every time he went to the movie theater where the bland young man sold tickets.

Like the powerful coils of a serpent, the Communist party gradually strengthened its hold on the Afghan people. Even after the *coup* of '79, when Taraki murdered President Daoud and some thirty members of his family, many adopted a "wait and see" attitude and hoped for the best. Tired of broken promises and the slow progress made by the former president, the people were ready for a change.

And changes had come. Repression. Mass arrests. Bombings and senseless killing. It wasn't long before the Kabul regime found itself at war with its own people. Moscow privately cautioned Taraki and his "loyal student," Prime Minister Amin to move more slowly, but they refused to listen. "Those who plot against us in the dark will vanish in the dark," was Taraki's grim promise to the people.

Ahmad lived through the days and months following the *coup* partially cushioned from all the horror by the protective shell of youth and the comforting notion that these things always happened to someone else. Never in his wildest dreams, could he have imagined that one day, the alcoholic father of the young man who sold him movie tickets would be responsible for his own arrest and imprisonment.

Chapter 5

"The beautiful things in the garden are not only the flowers.
There are many thorns that make those flowers look even more beautiful.
You won't know all the secrets of the garden,
Unless your clothes get hooked on one of those thorns . . . "

— Indian poem

It was daylight when the soldiers dragged me to a large room full of tortured prisoners and threw my semiconscious body inside. After they left, one of the inmates got up and took my hand.

"Come here," he said in a soft, lisping voice, and offered me the comfort of his own blanket.

I lay down on the blanket, only half aware of the young man who had given it to me. Turning my face toward the wall, I covered my head and burst into silent tears.

Some time later, a soldier entered the room, carrying a wooden baton. All the prisoners who hadn't been tortured recently were ordered to go to work in one of the yards. This left only a few men in the room, probably five or six besides myself. Glancing around, I recognized some faces from the day before. Sediq, the man whose eyes were injured from the torture. And the two young friends, Ibrahim and Quassim.

I was exhausted and wanted to sleep, but I couldn't sleep. I longed for quiet, but all around me I could hear people in the torture rooms crying, calling, swearing and screaming. Their pain was my pain.

After a while, Sediq crawled over to me and asked in a low voice, "Did you tell them anything?"

"No," I answered and he gave a satisfactory nod.

I lay in a stupor of shock and pain for several hours. The uncomfortable need to go to the bathroom eventually overrode the pain, but when I tried to get up, every bone and muscle in my body refused to cooperate. I finally managed to crawl on my hands and knees to the door, and, holding on to the wall, struggled to stand. After several unsuccessful attempts, I felt the support of someone's arms helping me to my feet. It was Ibrahim.

A soldier was posted just outside our room. I asked permission to use the bathroom, and he unlocked the door. There was no need for handcuffs, or an armed guard. It took all my strength and concentration just to walk.

The room where I had been taken after my torture was on the far east side of the prison. The bathrooms were some distance away in a courtyard on the west side.

Getting there was one of the longest, most painful walks of my life.

Even after reaching the place, I had another painful journey to make. The bathrooms were little more than primitive outhouses -- three holes in the ground enclosed by wooden sides in one corner of the yard. That ground was six or seven feet higher than the rest of the yard. To reach the outhouses, I had to climb a steep mound of hard-baked earth by means of small footholds.

I tried taking the first step and collapsed on my side with a groan. The pain was so intense I couldn't move. A moment later, I realized someone was trying to help me. Giving the stranger a grateful glance, I took his arm. One look at the young man's bruised face and blood-stained clothes told me he had also been tortured, but at least he could walk. Together, we inched our way up the rise to the outhouses.

When I finally got inside, I felt like a mountain climber who has reached the summit of his goal -- with one major difference. A climber pursues the sport because it's exciting and gives him a sense of accomplishment. I was feeling good because I had managed to keep the small sense of dignity and human feelings that were left to me.

The return trip wasn't nearly as difficult because my stomach was feeling much better. I was crossing the courtyard when I noticed a hose. Hurrying over to it, I turned on the faucet. Cold water gushed out in a welcome stream. I knelt down and splashed some on my face, then let it run over my head. The water soon turned red from all the blood. I rubbed a hand through my hair until the water ran clear once more.

When I got back to the room, Ibrahim greeted me with a big smile.

"You made it," he said.

"Yes," I answered with painful satisfaction.

There were a couple of dirty, bloody towels in the room. Ibrahim took one and started wiping my face and drying my hair.

Looking at his handsome face and big, dark eyes, he reminded me a lot of my brother Zoor. "Thank God, there are a few people like you left in this world," I told him.

"We've got to help each other, because no one else cares," he answered matter-of-factly.

I nodded, then asked if there was any food because I was starving.

"Every morning they bring a loaf of bread for everybody with some tea and sugar. Yours is still not touched," he said, handing me the bread and a glass of water.

I put a little sugar in the glass, stirred it with my finger and started to eat while Ibrahim went on talking.

"You know, I got married three months ago," he told me. "I have a very beautiful wife whom I love very much." After a deep sigh, he went on, emotion choking his voice. "Oh, I miss her! I miss her .... I miss my little sister and my mother. I don't know what's going to happen to them. They don't have anyone else but me to take care of them--" He broke off, his strong chin quivering and his dark eyes filling with tears.

"Ibrahim, with the help of Allah we're going to get out of here," I said. "Try not to worry too much. You know, one of our weak points is, we take things and people for granted. We don't appreciate them until we lose them."

I told him about my experience getting to the bathroom and how much I appreciated using the simplest thing. Looking down at the green cup in my hands, I said, "When I was washing the blood off my hair, the water looked red. Now, in this cup it looks green. The water doesn't have any color of its own, but when you put it inside something, it takes the color of that thing. Or if you mix it with another color, it will take on that color. Water doesn't have any taste, but when I was under the torture and they were throwing water in my face, it was the sweetest thing I could ever imagine. I've never felt or looked at water in this way. Maybe God is teaching us a lesson of appreciation for everything we have and see around us. That's probably why we're here."

There was a moment of silence between us and I found myself thinking about what I had said. It wasn't only to comfort Ibrahim. I think I was trying to convince myself that what was happening to us was for a reason, so I could make sense out of this horrible situation.

For a minute, Ibrahim just stared at the floor, his thoughts somewhere else, then he said, "I'm a musician. I went to India for four years to learn about classical music, which is like an ocean, there's so much to learn. First of all, you can't write it down, so you have to memorize every detail. But it's so fascinating! I came back just four months ago. Before I went to India, I was engaged and soon after I returned, I got married. Now my wife is pregnant and I'm in this place ...."

His eyes filled with tears once more, and I thought it might help if we talked about something less painful.

"My father loves Indian classical music," I told him. "He went to India many times on business trips and brought back some cassette tapes, so I know a little about that kind of music."

Ibrahim's face brightened and we began talking about different vocal artists and songs, giving our battered emotions a little rest from their wounds, along with our bodies.

That evening, the rest of the prisoners returned from their day's work. The young man who had given me his hand and his blanket approached me with a concerned look.

"Are you feeling better?" he asked.

"Well, I don't know if I would call it better ...."

"Yes, I know, but after a few hours you get your senses back. I saw you earlier when they brought you from that room. My name is Noor."

I gave Noor a closer look. His dark hair was thick and full, almost bushy, and he had a couple of days' growth of beard. He wasn't very tall, and he was wearing an Afghan outfit of loose shirt and baggy pants that had once been white.

"Your face is familiar," I said. Not only his face, but his lisping speech, or 'talking at the end of his tongue,' as Afghans say.

"I know you, too," Noor agreed with a nod.

"Where have we met?"

"I don't know, but I know I've seen you many times. Where do you work?"

"I'm a teacher."

Noor told me he worked for the government as an accountant and as we talked we discovered that we had both attended the same high school. Noor was a couple of years older than I, so he had been in a higher grade.

Sediq entered our conversation by introducing me to a pleasant-faced older man who was sitting next to him. "This is Arjung," he said.

"Arjung -- you mean, the artist?" I asked in amazement.

Sediq nodded and said with pride, "That's him."

Arjung was one of Afghanistan's finest artists and I had heard about his talents for years. In addition to being a painter, he was also skilled in calligraphy.

Arjung had a glowing face with the smooth, unlined skin of a child. His eyes were deep-set beneath thick, bushy brows. The only physical evidence of his age was his thinning hair, which was gray at the sides and balding on top.

We shook hands, and it seemed both amazing and ludicrous that I should be meeting a man whose talent I had admired for years in a torture-prison. Along with Arjung, Sediq introduced me to two others -- a young man somewhere near my own age by the name of Zaher, and an older fellow. Both men were pilots.

Some of their talk centered around a recent coup attempt which had failed. Sediq explained that he was supposed to fly a plane, but they were caught before it could happen.

Even though I was feeling a little stronger, it was difficult to concentrate on what was being said when I was in such pain. In addition to all the gashes from the beating, the skin of my fingers and toes was raw and burning where the electrical wires had cut into the flesh.

Noticing my discomfort, Noor told me to take off my shirt, then grabbed a towel and got it wet. "Don't wear anything for a while," he advised, cleaning the dried blood from the cuts on my back. "Just rest and let it dry."

"All right. You know best," I said, grateful for his help.

"Why did they punish you for so long?" he wanted to know.

"I'm not sure. They were asking me about my brother-in-law."

"Who's your brother-in-law?"

"Farid ... the doctor from Panjshir."

This information created quite a stir among the men around me.

"Are you really his brother-in-law?" Noor said with amazement, then his voice lowered to a confidential whisper. "You know what? He escaped this morning!"

The surge of happiness that rushed through me at this news, eased my pain even more than Noor's ministrations. Farid was alive! And free!

I lay down with a thankful sigh and slept for the first time in three days.

chapter 6

FOR SOME REASON the Investigators didn't call my name for a few days, and my wounds and I were having a little break. It didn't take long to learn the rules and routine of my prison life. Meals were brought three times a day -- tea and bread in the morning, soup for lunch and a little meat with rice in the evening. The food was quite good, but the portions were very small. No one ever felt full. We were always hungry. There were no washing facilities provided for inmates, just a single hose in the courtyard.

During the day, prisoners who were well enough to walk were taken to work; the rest of us stayed in that terrible room, suffering the effects of our own torture and all the while, listening to the screams and cries of those whose names had been called for the day shift.

One of the most difficult things for me to adjust to was having to think two or three hours ahead whenever I needed to use the bathroom. Well over a thousand prisoners were confined in *Sedarat* and there were only three small outhouses to meet one of the body's most basic needs. At first, I couldn't understand why this should be so. Then I realized it was yet another form of torture. Like me, other inmates were usually suffering and in pain when they made the long walk from their rooms to the outhouses, and then they had to wait in line with scores of other men. Very often, there were as many as two hundred men lined up, waiting to use the latrines.

One day, as I stood waiting my turn, I happened to notice an older man, about two or three people behind me in the line. He was tall and thin, with gray hair and round shoulders stooped with age. In spite of the man's wrinkled suit and dissheveled appearance, there was something undeniably distinguished about his bearing.

I didn't give him too much thought though, because the line was moving at a snail's pace, and the sun overhead was very hot. Little was said by anyone, each man intent on his own misery.

Moments later, the old man's humiliation became our shame as well. Patiently waiting in line, he hadn't uttered a word of complaint until suddenly, he was no longer able to control the demands of his bladder and bowels.

The incident became one of the main topics of discussion that evening. Everyone felt terrible that this old man should have suffered such indignity and embarrassment. The younger men all agreed that we should have shown more respect for his age, by asking him to go ahead of us in line.

Then one of the inmates, overhearing our conversation, inserted: "Do you know who that old man was? Gulaam Mohammad Farhad."

A shocked murmur went around the room. Gulaam Farhad was the former mayor of Kabul, and as such, he'd been my father's boss for many years. Although I had never met the man until today, I had heard much about him from my father, who praised Farhad for his honesty and fairness, as well as his progressive plans for the city. During his time as mayor, Farhad had worked hard to modernize Kabul with the addition of many fine buildings, schools and parks.

What kind of reward was this for all those years of public service? Standing in line with hundreds of beaten, tortured men, to use the latrine in a dirty courtyard.

If we'd known who he was, we would have insisted that Farhad go ahead of us in line. Admitting this, we felt even more ashamed, because we should have had more respect for any man his age, regardless of his position or who he was.

After talking about the problem, everyone agreed that from now on, we would make a point of asking to see if anyone needed to go ahead of us in line.

* * *

By the third or fourth day, I was feeling well enough to be angry. I thought of my brother Hafiz. Why did that idiot bring those men to Samad's house? He must have known they would take me, so why did he do it? The heat of my anger cooled when I realized the KhAD agents could have arrested my father or mother and tortured them in order to find me. Hafiz had no choice.

Still, I needed to blame someone or something. Why was this happening to me? My mind produced the logical reasons -- because of the Russians and the Communists -- but that didn't satisfy me. Then I thought, maybe I did something wrong.

As my eyes searched the square sky for answers, my memory brought back the day when I opened a closet in my mother's room and saw a large amount of money she had left there. I had never stolen anything in my life, but this time, I weakened to temptation's call and took a fifty *afghani* bill.

Everyone in my family thought my brother Zoor had stolen the money. They never expected me to do something like that. Zoor kept insisting that he hadn't taken it, but for one entire year he got the blame. Finally, I told my mother what I had done, but my confession couldn't erase the year that Zoor had been unjustly blamed for my actions. God knows how he must have felt during that time. Maybe that's why I'm going through this, I thought.

Or maybe I wasn't being a good Moslem. When I was younger, I would fast and pray with my family, but after I started going to college, I got busy and forgot about it. My father had always encouraged me to pray, but sometimes, I didn't pay a lot of attention. Maybe it was that ....

Near the end of my first week of imprisonment, the soldiers called my name again. My feelings of dread were magnified a hundred times, because now I knew what I was facing. Waiting in the torture room to supervise my interregation was the hulking figure of the big Afghan. This time, the torture lasted eight hours instead of twenty, and it was only the electricity, not the beating. The Investigators weren't being compassionate. Once the body is badly beaten, you don't feel the pain as much if they beat you again, but the electricity was something no one got used to.

During those hours of pain and degregation, the Investigators plied me with incessant questions about my brother-in-law, his friends and political activities. Telling them the truth, that I didn't know anything, only made them more determined. Eventually, the electrical fire jolting through my body took its toll and I found myself making up names and addresses. Anything to put an end to the torment.

That evening when the soldiers dragged me back to the room with the other prisoners, no one was the wiser. The Investigators had a few scraps of fabricated information and I still had no idea what it was they hoped to learn from me.

Lying in the crowded room, with the sounds and smells of torture and sickness all around, I felt totally abandoned.

Except for Ibrahim and Noor, none of the inmates really knew me or trusted me. For some reason, the fact that I was Farid's brother-in-law seemed to generate a lot of suspicion. A few of the men avoided me. Others were polite, but our conversation was safely centered on topics that weren't personal or political.

I wasn't sure who I could trust either, but as the days went on, there was one man that I found very intriguing. His name was Daghar-Wal (Colonel) Ibrahim. A short, chubby man in his mid-fifties, Daghar-Wal had silver hair and a thick mustache. Although he was dressed in traditional Afghan clothes rather than a uniform, his dignified manner as well as his title, told me that Colonel Ibrahim must be an important man in the Afghan army. Further evidence of this was the fact that the Colonel's name was called for torture more often than the rest of us.

Between torture times, he rarely spoke to other inmates, and his eyes were often focused on the ceiling or the window. Watching him, it seemed to me as if he knew an important secret, but didn't want to talk about it.

One night when the soldiers brought Daghar-Wal back after his torture shift, I noticed his forehead was bleeding from a deep cut. I wasn't in very good shape myself, but I crawled through the mass of sleeping men to where Daghar-Wal was lying, hoping to treat his injuries in some way. In Afghanistan, when someone is bleeding and there isn't any medical help available, people burn a piece of cloth and fill the wound with the ashes. I didn't want to burn anything that might attract the soldiers' attention, so I took out my pack of cigarettes. There were only a couple left, which I stuffed in my shirt pocket. Then, after crumpling the pack, I lit a match to the cardboard.

Daghar-Wal's eyes slowly followed the flame, as if it reminded him of his pain. When the cardboard had burned to ashes, I carefully filled his wound. I didn't have so much as a handkerchief to use as a bandage, so I tore a small strip from the gray sheet which served as bedding and tablecloth for the prisoners. A red stain slowly seeped through the cloth as I wrapped the makeshift bandage around Daghar-Wal's forehead, but at least the blood was no longer running down his face.

Daghar-Wal looked at me and whispered, "Why are you here?"

"I don't know. It has something to do with my brother-in-law."

"Who is he?" he asked.

"Dr. Farid."

When he heard the name, Daghar-Wal stared at me for a few seconds, then closed his eyes, pretending to go to sleep. I thought this was probably a polite way to get rid of me, so I crawled back to my own place.

Neither of us had occasion to speak to each other for a few days after that. Then one afternoon, I noticed the Colonel was pressing his eyes, rubbing his forehead and running his hands through his hair. I knew he must have a bad headache and asked if he would let me give him a massage. He didn't refuse, so I sat down behind him and began to massage his neck and shoulders.

This was a familiar duty that my brothers and I had performed for my father since childhood.

After a few minutes, Daghar-Wal's tight muscles began to relax beneath my fingers.

"I've been watching you for several days," he said quietly, "and I'm curious about something. Are you like Farid?"

"What do you mean?" I asked.

"Your brother-in-law is a good man," he told me. "He has good intentions, but he is lost. A Communist is still a Communist, whether he works for the Chinese or the Russians."

My fingers stiffened suddenly, and Daghar-Wal turned to face me. "You didn't know Farid was working for the Chinese?" he asked softly.

"I'd heard rumors," I admitted, "but he and I never discussed politics."

Daghar-Wal's wise gaze fastened on mine. "Farid is a good man," he said again, "but he's taking the wrong road to help our country." He sighed and turned around. "But it doesn't matter any more, because we're all going to lose our lives anyway."

After that, Daghar-Wal must have decided he could trust me, because we talked more often. During one of our conversations, he told me what had happened in Kabul prior to my arrest.

Several resistance groups, including one led by my brother-in-law, had joined in planning a *coup d'etat* against President Taraki's regime. As many of the groups had influential members in the army, the center of operations was at the old Bala Hissar fort overlooking the city. The uprising was scheduled for mid-day and the signal to go ahead was a pre-arranged disruption at the radio station where the transmission would be turned off for one minute at exactly twelve noon. This, Daghar-Wal explained, had been Quassim's and Ibrahim's job since they both worked at the station.

What the resistance didn't know was that three informers working for KhAD had infiltrated their group and reported the entire plan to their leaders. As a result, security was increased around the radio station and more troops were brought in. Ibrahim and Quassim were among those arrested and the signal was never given. The four main leaders, including Daghar-Wal and my brother-in-law, were captured, and the entire coup fell apart. Those who were waiting at the old fort finally went ahead on their own, and many were killed in the fighting which resulted.

At last I knew the reason for my arrest. I also knew why some prisoners had reacted to me with such distrust. No one in my family had any idea Farid was a Communist, let alone one of the leaders in something so far-reaching and dangerous as the recent coup. It was little wonder the Investigators were so desperate to discover what I knew about him.

The knowledge was sobering. Although I still loved and respected my brother-in-law, I had to agree with Daghar-Wal. Farid had taken the wrong road.

A day or two later, soldiers came to our room late at night with a list of prisoners to be executed. Along with the fear and dread of wondering whether my own name would be called, I felt a deep ache of sadness when I heard the soldier shout out Daghar-Wal's name.

Unlike other inmates who cried and hugged their friends goodbye, Daghar-Wal Ibrahim moved quietly around the room, shaking everyone's hand. All he said was, "*Khooda haffiz* ... may God protect us."

When he approached me, Daghar-Wal put his left hand on my arm and gave it a little squeeze. "It's time to leave now," he said softly.

As I looked into his face, his mustache widened and I saw his teeth for the first time. He was smiling -- a sad, ironic smile -- and there was no fear in his eyes. Daghar-Wal left the room and never looked back.

Later that night, I looked at the empty place where he used to sit and pictured the silver-haired colonel staring out the window the way he so often did. Somehow, I knew that the square sky had helped prepare him for this last trip of his life. I knew also that I would never forget his ironic smile, his sad eyes, and most of all, the way he pressed my arm. Daghar-Wal Ibrahim was a man of few words, but that one gesture held more emotion than anything he could have said to me.

Daghar-Wal left us with the dignity and bravery befitting a soldier. Thoughts of him inspired images of my country's flag rippling proudly in the wind. It was not the breeze alone that caused the flag to wave, but the heroic voices of all those who had given their lives for their country. I could almost hear the echoes of those sacrifices sighing in every breath of wind.

I bowed my head, silently hoping that those echoes would remember to honor the name of Daghar-Wal Ibrahim and his sacrifice for the flag of freedom.

Chapter 7

"Pain shared is half pain; happiness shared is double."
                              Old Afghan Saying

SOMEONE ONCE SAID that a discussion is an exchange of knowledge, while an argument is an exchange of ignorance. As my time in *Sedarat* lengthened from days to weeks, I found it fascinating to observe that there were never any arguments between the inmates. All we had was time, and with the exception of politics, there was a limitless possibility of subjects to discuss.

Many new prisoners arrived each day, most of them looking clean, neat and very frightened. But among those who had been arrested, we all knew there was the possibility that one of them might be an informer for KhAD. Especially if someone started asking a lot of personal questions, or tried to steer the conversation along political lines. Another warning flag was the fact that a few men stayed a week or more without being tortured, then quietly disappeared. Were they taken away to be executed, or had they been released before their presence could arouse more suspicion? We had no way of knowing.

Now I understood why my fellow inmates had stared at me the day of my arrival, and why no one said much until after I had been tortured. In a strange but very real way, those hours of pain were like a rite of initiation. Afterwards, you belonged.

Those arrested came from every station and walk of life -- soldiers, teachers, businessmen and farmers, religious leaders, doctors, even young students. In *Sedarat* we were all equals, united by the common bond of suffering.

I was grateful for the friendship of these men ... Sediq, Noor, Arjung, Quassim, and many others. But during those terrible weeks of torture and pain, the person I felt most comfortable sharing my thoughts and feelings with was Ibrahim.

The more we talked, the more we discovered that we had in common. Besides his love for philosophy and music, Ibrahim was fascinated with babies. I thought at first, this might be a painful subject for him, considering the fact his wife was pregnant, but just the opposite was true. Whenever our conversation turned to the topic of infants, Ibrahim would close his eyes and listen intently until I finished speaking.

"What were your feelings when Jossef was born?" he asked once.

"It's hard to put into words," I said, trying to block out the cries and moans of people in pain to reflect on that happier time. "When the nurse told me I had a son, I could feel the heat of joy and excitement rising from every cell of my body, melting frozen emotions I never realized I had. For nine months I'd tried to picture Jossef's face. I felt his kicks and his heartbeats ... I'd visualized him walking, talking and playing. Then, finally, I saw his face. It was a very unique experience. I went closer to him and started kissing his tiny hands and his chubby feet. I was totally elated by this miracle of life." I paused, then added, "Seeing my little son, I realized for the first time, how much my parents loved me."

Ibrahim's brown eyes were suddenly moist.

"Here is a word of consolation for you, Ibrahim," I said. "The anticipation during the months of pregnancy is wonderful, but after you see your baby's face and feel his soft skin ... once you hold that little infant in your arms ... it becomes the dearest thing in your life. Losing all that is not only painful mentally and emotionally -- it hurts physically. Being taken away from my son ... it's like a part of my soul has been cut out." I glanced down, trying to control the emotion that was causing my voice to tremble and break.

After a moment, Ibrahim said, "The few times I've had the chance to look into the eyes of babies, made me feel like I was transparent ... as if they were seeing through me, or looking at someone who was invisible to me. The only other occasion when I had similar feelings was when my father was dying. Standing near his bedside, I had the strongest impression my father was seeing someone other than the people who were gathered around him. Unfortunately, he couldn't talk -- otherwise I would have asked him to tell me what he was seeing." Ibrahim gave me a close look. "What do you think about that?"

"My mother used to say, there are two moments in our lives when we see the faces of the angels who accompany us through mortality -- the day we are born, and the day that we die. Perhaps that is who your father was seeing," I suggested. "Somehow, I don't believe that people make the journey back to God alone."

Ibrahim considered this, then agreed softly, "No ... not alone ...."

* * *

A few nights later, we were awakened around one a.m. by the harsh voice of a soldier screaming, "Get out of the room! Everyone get up and go outside!"

Hearts pounding with fear, we stumbled to our feet and did as he had ordered.

After all the inmates were assembled in the yard, the soldier stood in front of us with a bunch of papers in his hands.

"I'm going to read a list of people's names," he said. "As soon as you hear your name, get your belongings and wait in front of the cantina."

I was standing in front of Ibrahim, who whispered in my ear, "This is the list of people who are condemned to death. After midnight, any list is the end of our misery."

There were hundreds of people in the yard, but no one made even the smallest sound. We were all listening to the monstrous voice of the soldier as he read loudly and slowly the names of the guests and friends who had only a few minutes left of their visit in our little world.

In Afghanistan, many people have the same first name, like Mohammed, Mulah, Sayed, etc., but their middle and last names vary. As soon as the soldier read the first name, those men having that name were already seeing the flaming eyes of death in their imaginations.

The soldier was near the end of the list when I suddenly heard Ibrahim's name. I turned to look at my friend and saw the color leave his face.

With an emotional, trembling voice he said, "That's me."

Ibrahim went to our room to get his sport coat and I followed without saying a word. He took off the blue sweater he was wearing and gave it to me along with a key chain.

"If you get out of here alive, give this to my wife," he said. "Maybe she will smell my love for her in this sweater. You keep the chain, with my love and friendship."

He gave me a big hug and squeezed me against him. I could feel his body shaking, as he tried to stop himself from crying. Then he joined the others at the door.

From the window of our room, I watched the pale and petrified faces of the men who were leaving. Tears ran down my face and in my mind I was pleading, "Oh God, help them ... make it easy on them."

Afterwards, I lay staring at the ceiling, trying to remember Ibrahim's smiling face and all the things he had told me about his wife and sister, his mother and his friends, for the future.

A soft voice asked, "Are you missing your friend?"

"A lot," I answered, as Sediq moved beside me. "I can't get him out of my mind."

"The fear of cold water is much greater than being in it," he said. "Ibrahim's lucky. Tonight all his suffering is going to be over. We are the ones that have to face the pain and die a little every minute. You are probably the last one to share the final and deep feelings of his short life. Keep his memory alive and get on with what is waiting for you."

The next morning at eight a.m., my own name was called -- not for execution, but more torture. Instead of the usual torture rooms, I was taken to an older part of the prison I had never seen before. The soldiers escorted me into a dingy room where the Investigator was waiting, and I glanced around with a shudder. The walls, the floor, even the ceiling was stained with blood, and there was a terrible feeling in the room.

My Investigator was a different person than I'd had during other sessions, but the torture was the same. In fact, even harsher. By the time they took me back to the room with the other prisoners, it was six o'clock in the evening and my own blood had joined that of the nameless others in that horrible place.

This time, it was Arjung who took care of my wounds by getting the towels wet and cleaning off the blood. He even gave me a couple of aspirin which surprised me. When I asked where he got the pills, Arjung confided that he knew a soldier who sometimes brought him things from outside.

"Why were you arrested, Arjung?" I asked, trying to focus on something other than my body's pain.

"You remember hearing about the coup which failed?" he began. "I played a small part in that attempt. Your brother-in-law came to me some time ago and asked me to design a special coin which would identify members of the resistance. Someone told KhAD what I had done and I was sentenced to death. Then one of the Investigators suggested that instead of killing me, they should use my talent." He sighed and placed the towel's soothing wetness on my back. "Now I work for them. I write their slogans, paint their signs and draw pictures of their leaders."

I turned my head to look at Arjung's face. When he was sad, it was difficult to tell from his expression whether he was smiling or crying unless you saw his tears.

"I could never imagine myself doing these things for Communists," he went on, "but life is full of surprises. Someone told me that my family saw my name on the list of people who had been sentenced to death. They've already held my funeral and don't know that I'm still alive."

That night, my troubled thoughts as well as the pain kept me awake long after other prisoners had found momentary release in the haven of sleep.

I wondered what was happening to my family. Did they know I was alive? Or were they like Arjung's relatives, believing that I was dead? Farid may have gotten word to them, but most likely, it was too dangerous for him to try to contact any family members.

How had he managed to escape? Could that be a possibility for me as well? My mind toyed with the idea until I realized that escaping *Sedarat* would not bring an end to my torture. Even if I did get away, agents of KhAD were certain to arrest some other member of my family, probably my father. Being the cause of his death or imprisonment was far too great a price to pay for my own freedom.

Yet, what other choices did I have? At the moment, all I could see for myself was more pain and more torture. Perhaps Sediq was right when he said that Ibrahim was the lucky one.

During the next few days my depression deepened, reinforced by the constant misery all around me. I hadn't realized how much strength and support Ibrahim's friendship had given me against the horrors of *Sedarat*, until it was taken away. The loss of my friend, combined with the physical pain from that last torture session, made everything seem worse -- the flies and the filth, the smell of sickness and death, and the constant screams and cries coming from the torture rooms.

Feelings of despair clouded my heart and mind with such suffocating blackness that I finally reached the conclusion there was only one way out. Suicide. The soldiers were probably going to kill me anyway. Why not make it easy on myself? I searched the darkness in my mind for ways to accomplish this, and finally came up with a plan. The soldiers were bound to call my name again fairly soon, and when they did, I would try to grab one of their weapons. If I did that, I was sure they would shoot me. Meeting death in this way seemed much kinder than the hell I was going through.

The decision made, I began preparing myself mentally to make the attempt the next time my name was called for torture.

Chapter 8

"Memories are like singing cadences of the waves
in the deepest ocean of our emotions.
Caressing our colorful, exciting and most profound feelings,
they bestow upon us the wings to fly,
or the reasons to cry."

Sayed Ahmad Sharifi

ON FRIDAYS THE prison doors were locked and nobody worked, which gave the prisoners a little freedom. Inmates could walk around the yard, talk to each other and visit. On this particular Friday, I hadn't recovered enough from my last torture session to go outside. Besides the beating, my toes were badly infected where the electrical wires had burned through the skin.

I was sitting by the window, watching the men in the yard when I suddenly recognized the face of my brother Hafiz. He was looking around as if he were searching for someone and I knew that someone was me. I was overjoyed to see my brother, but not in this place. In my mind, I could picture the frightened faces of my family and the terror they must have gone through when those butchers from KhAD had arrested him.

Hafiz and I were actually half-brothers since he was the son of my father's first wife, but we had always been close. I considered him my friend and teacher as well as older brother. When I was growing up, he had been the one to explain the various changes in my body, and tell me a little about sex. Hafiz loved poetry and music and was by nature, a gentle, sensitive man. So sensitive, that I knew how much it would upset him if he saw me in my present condition. That and that alone kept me from calling out to him.

I sat by the window for over an hour, hoping to get a message to my brother. Finally, one of the prisoners returned to the room. I asked if he would please do me a favor and tell Hafiz that his brother was fine -- that he couldn't see me right now, but would in a few days.

Before I had the chance to see my brother again, a list came the following afternoon and Hafiz' name was called. Since it was still early in the day, I didn't think they were going to kill him.

There were different times during the day when the soldiers brought the list and each had its own significance. If the list came between nine o'clock at night and midnight, as it had with Daghar-Wal and Ibrahim, it almost always meant death. If the list was read between four in the afternoon and seven at night, that meant prisoners would be transfered to Pol-i-Charkhi, the big prison. And if a list was brought in the morning, it meant freedom. Sadly, other than calls for torture, there were rarely any names read in the morning. In Hafiz' case, I had the feeling that chances were very good he would be taken to Pol-i-Charkhi.

My brother's departure left me with a great sadness and strong memories of him and my family. Especially, my son Jossef. That night, I looked at the square sky from our window and said softly, "Please, God ... let me see him for one more time before anything happens to me."

Sometimes, when people talk to God with a burning and humble passion from the deepest part of a broken heart, they feel His answer. And I knew what His answer would be for me: *Have patience. I feel your pain.*

With this feeling in my heart and a great desire to see my family one more time, the pillars of my determination to make a drastic move began losing their strength. Thoughts of suicide faded, and from that moment, I felt prepared for anything I had to face.

I was under torture for another four weeks, but every time I felt weak, I concentrated on hearing the laughter of my family and friends, and I tried to talk to them in my mind. In other words, I was escaping prison. I was living in the past or in the future.

Before, when the Investigators had tortured me, I made up stories and created names and addresses, hoping to satisfy them. It usually took a few days to find out I was lying, then the Investigators would call my name again. Now I was determined not to tell them anything.

During the hours of electrical torture I had pain all over my body, yet I couldn't feel the pain. I was becoming indifferent to it. The Investigators asked me all kinds of questions, shouting and swearing and calling me names, but still, I remained silent. Finally, they realized they weren't going to get anything else from me, and left me alone.

In the weeks which followed, my physical torture was over, but the psychological and emotional torture became even more painful than the physical. Every time I heard the screams and cries of people going through torture, a sharp pain would shoot through my head, because I knew exactly how it felt. My stomach was often upset, and I had headaches that wouldn't go away.

At night I had terrible nightmares where members of my family were beaten, tortured and killed. Often, I woke up in a cold sweat. Even during the daytime, my imagination went wild. I felt as if I were losing my mind. Fortunately, my body recovered from the torture fairly quickly, and the soldiers started taking me to work in the yard.

Every morning promptly at seven, a soldier whose name was Awaz, arrived to wake us up. After we had eaten our breakfast of sugared tea and bread, Awaz shouted for us to stand in a line and follow him outside.

A tall man with a bony build, Awaz had a shaved head, cruel slits for eyes and a large, hooked nose that was always running. His mouth was running as well, in a continual stream of filth and profanities. Of all the guards, Awaz was the one most hated and feared by the inmates.

Awaz carried a long wooden baton which he was fond of using without warning. If an inmate made the mistake of talking back, or didn't respond to orders as fast as Awaz thought he should, Awaz would quickly demonstrate how talented he could be in using that baton.

One of the most painful examples of this was the time the soldiers brought three young brothers into our room. The eldest was only in his early twenties and the other two were still in their teens. The following morning, Awaz arrived at his usual time to take us to work. The oldest brother had been very ill during the night, and his only response to the order was a quiet moan.

Awaz was furious and started beating him with the baton. The young man's screams soon brought the warden who proceeded to make him an example for anyone else who might not feel like going to work. The warden stood over the youth, shouting for him to get up. Before he could make an attempt, the warden gave him a vicious kick and Awaz joined in the fray.

The rest of us watched in helpless anguish, as the young man was kicked from one side of the room to the other.

I glanced away from the brutal sight, and noticed his teenage brothers standing close together, clutching each other's hands. Their eyes were squeezed tightly shut, but I could see the young men's anger and pain in the form of silent tears which ran down their cheeks.

Somehow, the eldest brother summoned the strength to get to his feet. But now, besides being ill, he had several bruised or broken ribs to contend with. Pale and in pain, he staggered out of the room with the rest of the inmates.

Awaz never had an occasion to use his baton on me. The moment I heard his gruff voice in the morning, I would be up and ready for work in no time.

Behind the courtyard, was a large area where prison officials were adding more rooms to house inmates. My particular assignment was to throw bricks to the Mason. A short man with chubby cheeks and big hands, he always wore the same dirty hat pulled over his dark hair.

One afternoon while we were working, he asked where I was from.

"Baghebala," I replied.

"Oh, I know somebody from Baghebala. His name is Zoor. He's a good boxer and has his own boxing club."

"Zoor is my brother," I told him.

After giving me a closer glance, the Mason nodded. "Yes, I can see some resemblance. A couple of years ago when Zoor won one of his boxing competitions, me and him and a bunch of guys were driving a truck all over the place screaming his name." He grinned at me and said proudly, "Your brother's a good friend of mine. You tell me if you need anything, and if it's in my power, I'll get it for you."

"There is something," I said. "If you could go to my family and tell them I'm okay ... and maybe bring me a picture of my son."

The man nodded. "I'll do what I can."

The next morning, I didn't need any prodding to be up and going to work. It was all I could do to contain my eagerness. When I finally spotted the Mason in the yard, he greeted me with a big smile.

"I have some good news for you. Everybody in your family's fine. I couldn't get more information because Zoor's out of town and no one else knows me. They probably thought I was a KhAD agent and didn't trust me. But your father gave me a hundred *afghanis* to bring to you, and your wife gave me a picture of your son."

He slipped me the money and the picture and I quickly put them in my pocket before Awaz could notice anything.

"Thank you .... You don't know what this means to me."

The Mason gave me a pleased smile, then walked away, while I picked up more bricks and went back to work.

I didn't dare take the picture out to look at it as long as I was working. But out of excitement and impatience, I found myself working faster and faster, as if my speed could make a difference in the eternal seconds of my longest day at work.

By the time the day was over, my fingers were raw and bleeding from throwing God knows how many bricks. After washups, I tore a few pieces of cloth from the bottom of my shirt and wrapped them around my bloody fingers. Then, back in our room at last, I took the small black and white photo from my pocket.

Jossef was only a few months old in the picture. He didn't have much hair, but he had big, beautiful eyes and round fat cheeks.

I stared at the photo for hours. It brought back so many things. The feeling of Jossef's warm, chubby body sitting astride my shoulders when we went for walks in the park near our home. His wet kisses. The smile that would light up his dark eyes whenever I came home. Even the night he was born ....

I had just returned from a month-long job as guide for a group of tourists, when my family told me that Zarghuna had gone to the hospital to have the baby. Without stopping to change clothes or do anything else, I rushed to the hospital. The nurse in charge assured me that my wife was fine, but the baby hadn't been born yet.

In Afghanistan, husbands aren't allowed to be with their wives during labor and delivery, so I joined the rest of the expectant fathers in the waiting room.

A little while later, the nurse returned and approached me with a big smile on her face. "Mr. Sharifi ... you have a son."

A son! The news filled me with so much happiness, I threw my arms around the young woman and kissed her on both cheeks. Hugging strangers, especially women, is not considered proper behavior in Afghanistan, but the nurse didn't seem to mind.

Hugging her wasn't enough. I had to do something else to express my gratitude and joy. Grabbing my wallet, I took out a fat bundle of *afghanis* and handed it to the stunned nurse. Ordinarily, I wouldn't have had so much money, but the tourist agency had paid me in cash for my month's work.

The young woman stared at the stack of *afghanis* in her hand, her eyes and mouth wide with amazement.

I laughed and hugged her again. I had a son!

Smiling down at the photograph of my little Jossef, another memory suddenly nudged my consciousness -- the night I had looked at the square sky and prayed that God would allow me to see my son one more time. I remembered the peaceful answer that had burned in my heart. *Have patience* ....

A photograph might not be as wonderful as holding Jossef in my arms, but all the same, I knew my prayer had been heard. And I knew I must continue to do my part. I must have patience if I wanted to see my son and my family again.

Chapter 9

"From the strength of my tears, my eyes become like clouds,
Now my life story is known to nature;
Whenever I see these beautiful flowers,
I think of those beautiful faces and beautiful hearts
that are under the ground...."

Indian Poem

I HAD BEEN working for the Mason only a few days when Arjung approached me with a surprising offer. The warden had asked him to do some extensive painting in the Investigators' offices, and to get the job done faster, he told Arjung to choose two inmates to assist him. Arjung asked for Quassim and me.

The painting involved more than adding another coat of whitewash to the prison walls. First, Arjung would sketch an elaborate outline of various Communist slogans and sayings, after which, Quassim and I had the task of filling them in with paint. Slogans like: "Long Live Lenin!"

"Long Live Taraki!" and "Long Live the Revolution!" could already be found in offices and torture rooms throughout the prison. Now, it would be our privilege to add more of these literary masterpieces to the walls.

Considering our present situation, I couldn't help seeing the irony of such statements as: "The people of Afghanistan are united to take their destiny in their hands and change it for the better with the help of our friendly neighbor Russia." Or the stirring pledge: "We are ready to drain our blood for the road to Communism. All the imperialistic countries of the world with their local puppets, are united to weaken the pillars of our revolution, but with the support of our faithful army and our Russian friends, the triumph will soon be ours."

More often than not, the slogans had several misspelled words and the grammar was terrible.

The Investigators gave Arjung keys to their offices and instructed him to lock the door and not let anyone in while we were working. This situation worked out very well, because Arjung usually brought a big pot of tea and lots of candies in his pocket. With the door locked safely behind us, we would sit down for an hour or so, drinking tea, talking, and eating candy before going to work. Most of our talk was gossip about the Investigators whom we called all kinds of names and every swear word we could imagine.

Quassim was especially vocal in boasting about what he would like to do to the Communists, and how he would change things if given the opportunity. Quassim was a likeable man, educated and always polite, but there was something about him that puzzled and disturbed me at times.

He and Ibrahim had both worked for the radio station and should have been equally guilty in the eyes of the Communists. Why then, was Quassim still here while Ibrahim had been taken? And why was Quassim's name called so seldom for torture compared to men whose crimes were far more innocent?

I did know that he came from a very rich family, and his father had powerful friends, while Ibrahim had nothing. Was it money and his father's influence that kept Quassim alive?

Although I liked Quassim very much, there were times when I found myself silently questioning his motives.

"I have a joke for you," he said one day, smiling at Arjung and me. "A great meeting was called for the presidents of all the countries in the world. Each president was asked to bring a fruit or vegetable that was the symbol of their country. Then, after they arrived at the meeting, an announcement was made that the presidents had to take what they had brought and shove it up their ass. Fidel Castro brought carrots, and when the head of the United Nations saw him, Castro was laughing and crying. The man asked why he was laughing and crying. Castro answered, 'I'm crying because it hurts. And I'm laughing because I just saw Breshnev come in carrying a watermelon.'"

Jokes like this were our only means of revenge against the men who had imprisoned us. We made fun of the way they talked and the way they walked so proudly with their hands in their pockets, thinking they were the symbols of goodness, the gods of destiny, and the real patriots who were trying to help the poor people of Afghanistan.

What those Investigators refused to realize was the fact they had sold their country to the bosses of the Kremlin, and now they were torturing and killing the very people they were supposedly trying to save.

One day, it happened that I was left alone to paint an Investigator's office while Arjung and Quassim worked in another room. Although I enjoyed the companionship of my friends, being by myself for a few hours was a rare treat.

I dipped my brush in the can of red paint and began with the places I could reach easily, thinking I would need a small ladder or something to stand on to paint the rest. I glanced around and noticed a chair behind the Investigator's desk which would suit my purpose. As I grabbed the back of the chair, my gaze focused on a large stack of files sitting on the desk. Slowly, I set the chair back down, unable to take my eyes off those files.

The heat of curiosity and fear rushed through my veins. I was so nervous, my teeth started chattering. Trying to stop their shaking, I pressed the palm of my right hand beneath my chin and my fingers to my lips. I pressed down even harder as curiosity and fear waged a battle inside me. Moments later, I realized my hand was glued to my mouth because of all the paint that had dripped through my fingers. I pulled my hand away with a muttered, "*Why!* --

Ouch!" and discovered several hairs from my mustache glued to my fingers.

For some reason, that quick, sudden pain helped curiosity conquer my fears. I wiped the paint off my hands, then, like a small mouse looking around a trap for signs of danger, I peered out the office window to see if anyone was close by. The yard was empty. I put my ear against the wall, the door and even on the floor, listening for sounds that someone might be outside the room. When I felt it was safe, I pulled the large sheet of protective plastic closer to the desk, thinking if someone did open the door, I would at least be closer to my work.

Then, after giving the door and window one last check, I reached for a file. My heart was pounding as I lifted the front cover. The information inside was all handwritten. God knows where these people went to school. They had the worst handwriting I'd ever seen. It looked like someone dumped a bunch of ants inside an ink bottle, and then let them walk all over the pages. In spite of my nervousness, I had to smile. The writing was so bad that even the pen would die laughing at the end of the page. Maybe those pens were laughing to death, I thought. That was probably why the color of ink changed two or three times on the page.

It took some time to read and make sense of the first few lines because the Investigators used a lot of codes and numbers I wasn't familiar with. Following this were several pages of detailed information concerning the prisoner -- names of his relatives and friends, his education and workplace, a description of the investigation and the kinds of torture used, along with questions asked and answers given. On the last page, the Investigator wrote his comments and opinion regarding the prisoner. At the bottom of this page was the final decision of the President of KhAD.

I stared at the last page of that file, where the words: *Hedaam shawad* -- Sentenced to Death, had been written in bright red ink. Never before had two words had such immense meaning, and such a physical and emotional impact on me. My stomach started to churn and the writing on the page blurred before my eyes.

I set the file back down with shaking hands, then leaned against the wall to light a cigarette. What if the next file is mine? I asked myself. My eyes were focused on the desk in front of me, but in my mind, all I could see were those two words written in red ink, looking like the flaming eyes of death itself.

A sharp, burning pain between my fingers jerked me back to reality. The cigarette was finished and I had smoked only one puff. I crushed the butt, then walked over to the window and stared out at the dirty courtyard. "You will never get out of here alive," I said in quiet despair.

During the next three hours, I went through all the files in that office, but I couldn't find mine. Of the fifty or so that I read, at least ninety per cent of them had death sentences written on the last page. I was so engrossed in my reading, I almost didn't notice a scuffling sound outside the room. Footsteps!

At first, I was so petrified I couldn't move. Then my whole body began to shake. When I saw the door knob turn, I threw the file I'd been reading beneath the desk and jumped up to my place of work. In my haste, my foot bumped against the can of paint and knocked it over, spilling red paint all over the sheet of plastic.

Seconds later, an Investigator entered the room and asked if I was doing a good job. I was so frightened, I couldn't utter a word. The man glanced at me, then the spilled paint, assuming my nervousness was because of the mess I'd made.

"You weren't told to paint the carpet, only the walls," he said sarcastically. He took a second look at my face and began to laugh. "And don't eat the paint," he added. "It's more expensive than food."

As he turned away, I thought to myself: *Don't worry. No paint on earth can cover all the innocent blood that stains these carpets.*

Still laughing, the man left the room, locking the door behind him.

Sometimes God helps us in a very mysterious way. I knew if I hadn't spilled that paint, one glance at my face would have told the Investigator what I was up to. And once he discovered that, I had no doubts the words: **Hedaam shawad** would be written in red ink on the last page of my file.

The first thing to greet me at the end of my work day were the faces of roommates whom I now knew had been sentenced to death. Realizing they would be our guests for perhaps another minute, a day, or a week, my perception of them changed completely. Their laughter, their voices, their whole existence suddenly attracted my attention, as if I were trying to paint them indelibly into the pages of my memory.

That evening, the knowledge of the files turned my mind into a battlefield. Should I tell them or shouldn't I? If I told my fellow inmates about their death sentences and they survived the shock, they might attempt something drastic. If they tried to escape, I was certain they'd be caught. Since Farid's escape, and another incident where an inmate had gotten out by hiding under a construction truck, prison security had been much tighter. More lights had been added, weak places had been fortified, and there were more guards with machine guns watching the halls and doorways.

Yet, if I didn't tell my friends and their names were called, I would still blame myself, because perhaps they would have had some small chance of escaping if they had known. I didn't know which was worse.

During dinner that night, all I could do was watch the men eat and offer them my food. Afterwards, I sat close to them and tried to share a few thoughts that I hoped might be of some help.

"We are all mortal," I said. "Only God is eternal. If we die for a good cause, God might forgive us for the sins and mistakes that we have committed. Nothing is given to us for free in this world or the next. Maybe this is a way that God wants to give us the opportunity to sacrifice in this life for the next one. Our families, our friends, even our land will know that we didn't die in vain, and our memories will stay with them for eternity ...."

In the days and weeks which followed, I worked very fast to get my painting jobs done, then I would find the files in that particular office and start reading. God knows how many death sentences I saw. Not only did I learn the sad destiny of many people that I met in *Sedarat*, my work also gave me an intimate knowledge of the prison. Every hallway, every office and every room became increasingly familiar -- like a blueprint written in my mind.

One Friday, I was enjoying a few minutes of sunshine in the yard, when a prisoner by the name of Ashraf hobbled over to me. In better days, he had been a teacher at Poli-Technic University. Now, Ashraf had steel bands around his wrists and ankles which were connected by a thick metal chain. The chain wasn't long enough to allow him to stand upright, so the poor man was forced to walk in a backbreaking stoop. As a result, the skin of his wrists and ankles was raw and bleeding.

Ashraf sat down beside me and confided that he was going to try to escape. Knowing that I had some knowledge of the prison, he asked for any information that might help him with his plan. I drew some pictures in the dirt, showing him the way out, but at the same time, I felt obligated to offer a few words of caution. I told Ashraf how prison defenses had been fortified, showed him where the soldiers were, and all the guards with machine guns.

"It's up to you," I said finally, "but I wanted you to know it's very dangerous."

Two days later, Ashraf's name was called late at night and the soldiers took him away. Guilt and remorse kept me awake for hours after he had gone. Should I have encouraged him more with his plans to escape? At least then, he might have had a slight chance to live. Now it was too late.

During all those weeks of reading the files, I never told anyone what I knew -- except one doctor.

One morning, I was waiting in line for the bathroom, when I noticed the man standing in front of me. He looked very sad and sick, yet he was still polite enough to tell me that I could go before him if I needed to.

"No, I'm fine," I said, then added in a low tone, "Don't turn around. Just listen to what I have to tell you. Your name is Habib. You are a doctor in Mazar. You were arrested five months ago in your office."

I went on to tell him every little detail that I had read in his file. "Soon they will take you to Pol-i-Charkhi for another four months," I said, "and after that, you'll be set free."

After listening to me, Dr. Habib knew that all the details were true. He was so overcome, he could not control himself. He turned around and started kissing my hands, all the while telling me, "I will never forget this. I thought they were going to kill me."

Sure enough, two days later the soldiers came with a list of names in the afternoon, and the doctor's name was one of those called. I watched him as he was leaving. Habib must have saluted me with a big smile more than ten times.

Although I was very happy for him, it didn't take away the pain of knowing there were hundreds, even thousands of others who were not so fortunate. As time passed, I often wondered what I would do if I found my own file and saw the death sentence written at the bottom of the page. The more files I read, the more I found myself changing. Everything around me seemed to be changing as well. Even the friendly square sky and beautiful stars began playing deadly games with my imagination. At night I would see the victims' names and those horrible words, *Hedaam shawad* written across the sky. In my mind, I saw their bodies hanging from ropes. Others were riddled with bullets and blood. And most horrifying of all, I saw people being buried alive in a huge pit, while bulldozers made sure all the entrances were sealed, to prevent the angel of life from kissing their dying lips that were so thirsty for a breath of heavenly air.

Late one night, I was struggling to remove these terrifying thoughts from my mind, when a soldier's loud voice called us out into the yard.

After we had lined up, he began shouting the names of various inmates. I was amazed to know so many of them. As I listened to the names of those invisible heroes, my brain was rapidly revising the files. I thought about their so-called crimes and asked myself: What did they really do? My answer was always the same. They tried to stop the Russians from killing and raping their women and children. And the worst crime of all -- they loved their country.

Early the next morning I woke up in a cold sweat. My chest was tight and I was having a hard time breathing. All night long I'd wrestled with nightmares about those inmates I could no longer see or hear.

The stars were still shining in that beautiful square sky when I got up and joined the other prisoners who had assembled for morning prayers. Next to the warden's room, there was an open space surrounded by three high walls. It was darker, but cleaner than the rest of the courtyard. This humble place became our mosque, a place of refuge where inmates would gather morning and evening to pour out their devotions to God.

Kneeling there in the dark courtyard, the peaceful thought came to me that someday, out of the hole where these victims were buried, there would grow the wildest and the reddest flowers to remind the world that no matter how deep the devil tries to bury innocent people, he will never be able to cover their smiling faces.

That morning I made the decision to stop reading the files, because I wanted to keep the flame of the candle of hope burning.

chapter 10

"The more I fell down, the more I learned how to take the hand of someone else who was falling..."
                                    Afghan saying

ON A WARM September day, Ahmad dipped his brush into a bucket of red paint and began filling in the scripted letters Arjung had sketched on the office wall. After several hours' work, his arm ached, his back ached and he was sick and tired of painting the names of Lenin, Breshnev and Taraki.

A knock on the door brought his painting to a sudden halt, and a moment later a young guard entered whom Ahmad recognized as one in charge of food for the prisoners.

"You're wanted by some Investigators in the main office," the guard said, instructing Ahmad to leave his job for the time being and come with him.

Ahmad put the brush down and wiped his hands on a rag, unable to control the rapid pounding of his heart.

What did it mean? Was he being called for more torture after all this time?

As the two young men walked down the hall, the guard glanced at Ahmad with an expression that could almost be called friendly. Ahmad's answering look was slightly bewildered.

"My name is the same as yours," the guard explained with a smile. "My name is Ahmad, too. Ahmad Shah."

"Oh, really? Well, that's good. At least we have our names in common."

"Didn't you live in Baghebala?" the guard went on. "I remember seeing you in the soccer field a few times."

Ahmad nodded absently, his nerves growing more tense the closer they got to the main office.

Seeing his prisoner's worried face, the guard added, "Don't worry. It's not torture. I can tell you that much."

Whether it was his tone or his direct way of speaking, Ahmad had the feeling the young man was telling him the truth.

In the main office, a group of Investigators had gathered to discuss the files and "crimes" of their newest victims. Among them was a distinguished, well-dressed man from the Department of the Interior. Nazir Kazimi leaned his tall frame against the edge of a table, his attention focused on the file in his hands. As the guard entered with Ahmad, Nazir set the file down, his eyes making a quick assessment of the prisoner. "Sayed Ahmad Sharifi?"

"Yes, sir." Ahmad nodded respectfully. He recognized most of the Investigators in the room, having painted their offices. Others had a more painful association, as they had been assigned to his case during the early weeks of his imprisonment. The man who addressed him now, Ahmad had never seen before.

"I read in your file that you speak French," the man said pleasantly.

"Yes, sir."

"Then perhaps you can help us. We need a translator here." Kazimi indicated a young man and woman who were handcuffed and sitting to his right. "This couple were caught in a place they weren't supposed to be, and we have a problem communicating with them. We'd like you to find out what they were doing there. Right now, we're preparing some questions in writing. You'll need to translate the questions for them and write down their answers."

Ahmad glanced at the man and woman sitting nearby. They appeared to be in their late twenties, and were dressed in jeans and the silk-embroidered shirts popular with tourists. For a moment, Ahmad was so excited to see new faces that weren't beaten and tortured, he totally forgot himself. Eagerly approaching the couple, he held out his hands to them.

The shock and fear in their eyes suddenly reminded Ahmad what he must look like. Wild black hair and beard, both overly long. Dirty, disheveled clothes.

The young couple's fear melted into relief as Ahmad's rich voice greeted them in their own language. It was awkward though, trying to shake his hand when both his and theirs were confined in handcuffs.

Quietly observing the situation, Nazir Kazimi gestured to one of the guards. "Remove the cuffs."

"Do you speak French?" Ahmad asked the young couple, as the guard removed their handcuffs.

"*Oui*. We are both from France," the man replied, shaking Ahmad's hand.

Kazimi turned to pick up some forms lying on the desk, then handed them to Ahmad. "There are some questions here that we'd like you to translate and have them answer."

Ahmad gave the papers a cursory glance, seeing spaces for names, passport numbers and other pertinent information.

"You won't be able to complete all the forms right now, though, since it's lunchtime," Kazimi went on, giving his watch a glance. "Tell the couple they can have an hour off. Afterwards, the guard will bring them back and we'll talk." Kazimi paused, then added in the same pleasant tone, "As long as you're here, you might as well have lunch with them," he said and signalled the guard.

After leaving the main office, Ahmad Shah escorted Ahmad and the French couple to a room Ahmad had never seen before. They were about to enter when the guard touched Ahmad's sleeve. "Be careful what you say in there."

Ahmad's eyes met the guard's in wordless understanding, realizing the place was probably bugged. What had seemed at the time to be a generous gesture on the part of the official, now made chilling sense. If the Investigators suspected the French couple were spies, they probably hoped the normalcy of eating lunch with a young man who spoke their language would encourage some candid conversation.

After the guard had gone, Ahmad glanced quickly around the small room. A wooden table and some chairs stood near the center, and there was a delapidated couch against one wall. Hanging on another was a framed picture of President Taraki. Without a word, Ahmad began looking around the room to see if he could discover anything unusual. He even checked behind the picture, but couldn't find any holes or other evidence to indicate they were being watched. Still, after the guard's warning, Ahmad suspected the Investigators must have a recorder or microphone hidden somewhere.

He made a few casual comments to the French couple, at the same time gesturing for a pen or pencil. When they didn't understand, he finally resorted to whispering in the woman's ear. "*Avez vous un crayon?*"

Nodding, she emptied the contents of her purse on the table. In addition to a wallet, two paperback books and the usual feminine belongings, Ahmad discovered a pad of paper, some ink pens, a pencil and an eraser.

Taking the pencil and note pad, he scribbled in French: *Keep talking ... just keep talking, about anything except politics.* Ahmad showed the note to the man who nodded jerkily and began making conversation about the weather and whatever else came to mind.

Ahmad was impressed with his quick response and grasp of the situation. Although they were dressed like tourists, he suspected this French couple were more than that. Journalists, perhaps.

The woman took the pencil and wrote: *What is this place?*

Ahmad erased her words and explained: *This is a prison. This is the torture place and I think they suspect you are spies or something.*

The sudden fear washing over their faces said more than anything they could have told him.

Ahmad continued writing. *You're lucky you haven't talked to them yet, because if you talked to them and they proved something, you could be in a lot of trouble.*

The young woman gave him a sympathetic glance, then wrote: *What happened to you?*

Ahmad erased her question and answered simply: *I was beaten for political reasons.* He went on writing, telling the couple all about the prison, the torture and killings, the Russians who helped supervise it, and whatever else might be valuable for reporters to know.

The sound of footsteps outside the room interrupted his writing. Ahmad quickly shoved the pencil and notebook into his pocket, while the woman gathered the rest of her belongings and dumped them unceremoniously in her purse. Seconds later, a guard entered with food on a tray.

Ahmad waited until the soldier had gone, then invited the young couple to help themselves to the food. Neither one had any appetite. The woman looked visibly shaken and could only sit, clutching her purse with white-knuckled fear. When Ahmad offered some bread to the man, he shook his head and slumped down on a chair.

Ahmad knew what they were feeling. The traumatic memories of his own arrest never faded from his mind. With renewed determination, he retrieved the notebook and started writing.

I know what they're going to do ... They're going to ask each of you certain questions and then they'll compare what you say. If your answers are different, you're in big trouble. Both of you make one story. Make sure that it is the same. I'll do my best to help you, but you need to trust me.

Aloud, he said, "The soup is very good. Have you had a chance to enjoy some of our Afghan food during your visit?"

The man took his cue and began talking about the *pilau* and delicious Afghan bread found at various restaurants, while the woman erased Ahmad's words and wrote in a trembling hand: *I trust you. Please help us.*

Ahmad smiled and gave her an encouraging nod, then started composing an alibi for the couple to give the Investigators. *Tell them that you read a book by Joseph Kessel called, "The Horsemen." After reading this book, you became very interested in Afghanistan and planned a vacation to see the country, because you wanted to know the people and the culture better ....*

After he had given all the instructions that he thought might help them, the young woman took the pencil and wrote: *What can we do to help you?*

Ahmad shook his head, then wrote: *Only God can help me now.*

The man reached into his pocket and took out some money, but Ahmad politely refused the offer. Then, taking the pencil, he told the woman that he would like very much to have one of her novels. She smiled and reached into her purse for one of the paperback books.

Ahmad glanced briefly at his treasure before hiding it under his clothes, and smiled his thanks.

The guard Ahmad Shah arrived promptly after the lunch hour to escort Ahmad and the French couple back to the main office, where the officials were waiting.

Ahmad had no difficulty translating the various questions on the typed forms. After the couple had given him their answers, he translated them into Dari-Persian for the Afghan officials. When the Investigators began asking him pertinent questions about the French couple's motives, he did his best to cover for them, giving the story they had agreed upon. Afterwards, he was ordered to sign his name and put his fingerprints on another form, testifying that what he'd translated was the truth.

The French couple were asked to sign the document as well, but when Ahmad explained this, the young woman refused, telling him she wasn't going to sign something she didn't understand. Ahmad sent her a silent look of approval, admiring the woman's courage as well as her intelligence.

After he had translated the contents of the document, both she and her companion signed the form. His usefulness to them at an end, one of the Investigators approached Ahmad with a pair of handcuffs, then summoned the guard.

As he left the office, Ahmad turned for one last look at the French couple, wishing he could do more, or at least say goodbye, yet knowing he must remain silent. A fragile moment of communication passed between the three, with only their hearts and eyes speaking to each other. When Ahmad's gaze met the woman's, he was moved by the glimmer of unshed tears in her blue eyes. Then the door shut behind him.

On their way back to Ahmad's room, the young guard glanced at the happy smile on his prisoner's face. "Do you know those people?" he asked, clearly puzzled.

"No, but it gives me a good feeling to think that I helped them," Ahmad answered. "You don't have to know people to love them."

The guard shook his head. "You're crazy!"

Ahmad smiled at him and said nothing.

Throughout the day, Ahmad kept the novel hidden under his clothes, knowing he would be beaten or worse if it were discovered. Not until late that night, did he dare take out his treasure.

Surrounded by sleeping, snoring prisoners, Ahmad carefully opened the book, turning the pages toward the sickly yellow light of the room's single overhead bulb. *Le Vol de Nuit*, or *Night Flight*, was a novel he'd been familiar with since his college days. Back then, he hadn't appreciated Antoine de St. Exubery's writing because the plot wasn't fast-paced or exciting enough to suit his tastes. Now, this simple story about pilots and their experiences provided a winged passageway out of the horror and suffering which surrounded him. The cries and screams of those undergoing torture seemed to fade, and he was lifted beyond the confines of the prison walls, into the expanse of a limitless night where men were free to soar above the earth.

The next morning, as Ahmad and his fellow inmates were eating their small ration of bread and tea, he noticed the guard Ahmad Shah gesturing to him from the doorway.

"Come over here," the guard called.

Ahmad got up and did as he asked.

"Here." The guard held out a small sack to Ahmad and said, "I know they don't feed you very well, so I'll bring you my bread every day."

Ahmad stared at the young man in surprise. "But what will you do?"

"I go home every night," Ahmad Shah answered with a shrug. "And I hate their food anyway, so you're welcome to it."

Amazed, Ahmad thanked him and took the sack. When he sat down and looked inside, underneath the bread he discovered a deck of cards. Ahmad couldn't believe his good fortune. First a book, and now a deck of cards.

Throughout the day, Ahmad's experience with the French couple and his conversation with the guard provided a pleasant diversion for his thoughts. In spite of Ahmad Shah's laughing response, something in the words *... you don't have to know people to love them ...* must have touched him. Ahmad committed the words to memory, feeling a warm peacefulness inside. The memory helped soften the sounds of torture, and the small novel hidden under his clothes offered the promise of escape for the evening to come.

Although he managed to keep the book hidden from the guards, withholding such a gift from his friends and fellow inmates was something Ahmad could not do. Especially since they were as starved for the nourishment found in a good book as he was. When they learned about the paperback novel, everyone wanted to read it. Ahmad was the only one in the room who could speak and read French, however, so he offered to read part of the book each night, translating the French into Dari-Persian. When Ahmad stopped reading, the men begged him to read just a little more, like small children asking for another bedtime story. Since the book wasn't very long, Ahmad tried to convince them it would be better if he read only a few pages at a time; that way, they could savor the experience as long as possible.

After the pages of the novel were closed, Ahmad lay on his side, staring at the square sky outside his window. A pensive smile touched his lips as his mind opened the pages of another book -- chapters of his life written in the colorful ink of memory. Reading the novel brought back the years he'd spent studying the French language -- teachers, tests, and the satisfaction of earning his degree. After months of searching, he'd finally secured a job teaching French at the same high school he attended. The position was only temporary, but Ahmad didn't mind. He had other plans. First, earning a scholarship and then, continuing his studies in France. He had always wanted to see Paris. For years, it had been a dream living inside him. And now he was in this place ... where every day was like the day before, a never ending nightmare.

Ahmad sighed and shifted position on the hard floor, feeling the smoothness of the book against his skin. He wondered if the French couple had been allowed to leave *Sedarat*. He hoped the alibi he'd suggested was enough to convince the officials to release them, but realized he'd probably never know what happened.

There was something about the woman -- the tears in her eyes, and her soft voice speaking the language that he loved so much -- that stirred the embers of another time ... the summer he'd been a tour guide and met a pretty French girl with long brown hair and tears in her blue eyes. *Angelique* ....

Chapter II

" ... In this life, a sweet memory has more truth in it than the whole happiness."
                                        Alfred de Musset

HOLDING A SIGN with the Tour number of Air Alliance, I waited at the crowded airport of Kabul. An attractive young lady wearing sunglasses and a big hat approached me and introduced herself as the tour leader. We talked for a few minutes, going over instructions for the tour, then I showed her where she could find the bus which would take the tourists to their hotel.

After all the luggage had been loaded and the tourists were seated in the bus, I introduced myself and asked them to please do the same. Eighteen men and women, all from France, told me their names. Since European names were difficult for me to memorize, I went down the aisle of the bus, writing each person's name on a piece of paper, along with a little trait of his appearance. There was the tall one, the skinny one, the doctor and his wife, and so on. At the end of the bus, I saw a shy young lady with blue eyes, long brown hair and rosy cheeks. Her long hair and the black tee-shirt she was wearing, made her eyes look like two candles burning in the dark.

With a very soft voice, she gently said, "My name is Angelique."

Beside her name, I wrote: *the angel face.*

Her companion on the journey was a good-looking, but somewhat arrogant young man by the name of Michel.

A few minutes later, we were on our way to the hotel. Excitement, along with some nervousness put thoughts of the *angel face* momentarily out of my mind. I was eighteen, newly graduated from high school, and this tour was the first time in my life that I'd had the chance to earn some money.

Late the night before, one of my schoolmates had come to my house, asking for a favor. Nadjib had a family emergency which prevented him from acting as tour guide for a group of French tourists, and wondered if I would take his place.

I told Nadjib I'd like to help him, but that I'd never been to any of the places on the tour and had no experience as a guide. My friend kept encouraging me and assured me the job was a "piece of cake," or, as they say in my country, "a glass of water."

After talking it over, I told Nadjib I would go. My parents both agreed that this would be a wonderful opportunity for me to see the country, as well as giving me the chance to earn some extra money. By this time, it was well after midnight. Nadjib and I hurried over to his house, where he gave me some information about my duties, the roads and his notes about the history of the various sites we were going to see.

Excitement and nervousness made it difficult to sleep that night. Early the next morning I went to the tourism agency where I was given instructions for the trip. The man in charge emphasized many times that it was my responsibility to get the tour to its destination before dark, unless I had a very good excuse. I left the agency weighed down with my new responsibilities and something else -- thousands of *afghanis*. In the hotels where the tour had reservations, all I had to do was sign for expenses, but many places were so remote there were no banks and checks weren't accepted. For such places, I would need to pay cash.

I had never seen so much money in my entire life. After stuffing the *afghanis* into the pockets of a new money belt which I wore inside my clothes, I headed for the airport, feeling like a chubby Asian Santa Claus.

Early the following morning we were on our way. The tourists were in high spirits, singing songs, laughing and telling jokes as we drove along the asphalt highway out of Kabul. The morning air was cool and the road was smooth.

I said nothing to spoil their mood, but I knew it wouldn't last long.

For our six-week adventure across Afghanistan, the tourists and I did not have the comfort of riding in a Mercedes Benz bus, like the one that picked them up at the airport. Instead, we were traveling in two off-road vehicles called *vaz's*. These sturdy Russian-made trucks had huge tires specially equipped to handle Afghanistan's "raw roads." Padded benches against the truck's metal sides provided seating, but there was no covering of any kind to protect the tourists from the wind, the dust and the blazing Afghan sun.

Besides the passengers, the back of each truck also carried large barrels of water and gasoline for the long journey.

By ten-thirty in the morning, the heat came and the singing stopped. That's when my job as tour guide and chief entertainer began. I told stories, jokes and gave information about the places we were driving through -- anything to keep their mind off the heat and the dust.

I was a little worried about my lack of knowledge where the roads were concerned, and soon discovered that the drivers knew even less than I did. Remembering Nadjib's adamant advice to never let the tourists know that I didn't know what I was doing, or they would panic, I devised a system to help keep us from getting lost. I told both drivers that whenever they didn't know which way to go, to make some excuse to stop and check something in the trucks. While they were doing this, I would get out and ask directions from someone in that particular village or area. Since none of the tourists spoke Dari or Pashtu, they thought I was just being friendly, and no one was the wiser.

Another test of my skills as tour guide was the tourists' constant curiosity about anything and everything. Until this trip, I had no idea French people were so curious. Some of their questions were very interesting, but others, I had no idea how to answer.

We would be driving through the middle of nowhere and one of them would see a couple of houses, or perhaps a cemetery.

"Whose house is this?" he would ask. Or, "What kind of people are buried there?"

The first time I was asked these questions, I had to get out my thinking pillow, which was my fist beneath my chin, then I would answer: "Those houses belong to my grandfather and his brother," or -- "my great-great grandparents and their relatives are buried in that cemetary."

Then there was the time I was asked in all seriousness, "Why is it, in some villages we see dogs chasing our trucks, and in others, we don't see any dogs?"

I couldn't stop laughing. Finally, I said, "Maybe people in this village eat dogs. That's probably why there aren't any."

The tourists knew I wasn't serious, and soon everyone was laughing.

Each evening after we arrived at our destination and the tourists were settled in their rooms, I would go out into the town or village, asking questions of my own, trying to find out what was there and learn what might be of interest to the people on the tour. The villagers were always very willing to help, even though I felt like a student doing some last minute "cramming" for a test.

The tour's first main stop was Bamiyan, a beautiful fertile valley where ancient civilizations once thrived.

Carved into the sandstone mountainside are the largest Buddhas in the world and many caves where Buddhist monks once lived.

That night, everyone was excited and in good spirits as we sat down at the long dinner table. Spread before us was a colorful variety of Afghan food -- all kinds of rice *pilau* cooked with lamb and vegetables, *bulani* -- delicious meatballs cooked with spinach, tomatoes and tantalizing spices, and so many kinds of *kabobs* I could hardly count them. Our hosts were especially anxious for the tourists to experience the varied kinds of delicious Afghan food, because for the next three or four days we would be driving through remote regions where there weren't any good hotels.

The large dining room was crowded with tourists from other tours as well our own. As I looked around to see if I knew any of the other guides, I spotted one of my French teachers from high school sitting at a small table with some friends. Monsieur Gilbert was a tall, strong man with wide shoulders, startling green eyes and long hair. I enjoyed his "hippie look" and his eloquent way of speaking, always choosing the most effective words to describe and enhance his point of view.

I got up and asked Monsieur Gilbert if he would like to join us at our table, which he did. After I had introduced him to the tourists, he sat down across from me and dived into his meal. The intense look on his face, the serious slant of his eyebrows and the hums he made through his nose while he was eating, were all signs of his passion for Afghan food.

After a moment, he asked me about our destination. I told him that we were going to Band-e-Amir, Jam, then Herat.

When he heard the word Jam, he set his fork down and with his eyes focused on his plate said, "Jam ... what a beautiful place." After a moment of contemplation, he glanced up at me. "I'm going to tell you about one of my experiences in that place."

My curious tourists leaned a little closer, eager to catch his every word.

"Three years ago, my teaching contract was over," he began. From childhood, I've loved challenges and seeing exotic places. And since I first came to Afghanistan, I've been obsessed with the idea of taking the Central Road during the winter, because no one dares travel through those snowy mountains and high deserts during that time of year. Finally, the time was right. I packed everything I thought I would need in my four-wheel drive Land Rover and left Kabul.

"It took me four times longer than usual, but I finally made it to Band-e-Amir. There I was ... all alone ... looking at those breathtaking natural lakes. I'll never forget that early morning, seeing the reflection of the sun, the snow and the sky on the surface of the lake. It looked peacefully blue, and almost solid -- like an island of lapis-lazuli set in the snow. Band-e-Amir is beautiful in summer, but at this time of year, it looked like a dreamland. I can still hear the chaos of the waterfalls, rushing down the changing faces of the ice." He paused a moment, his green eyes sparkling with the beauty of the memory.

"The next day, I was driving toward Jam. It was very cold and the road was full of snow, which made my trip much longer than I'd planned. Then something went wrong with my car. I tried everything I knew to fix it and finally gave up. I wasn't sure how far I was from Jam, but it was so cold and the snow was so heavy, I knew I wouldn't last long if I started walking. All I could do was stay inside the car and wait for a miracle."

My former teacher chose this moment to pause, and I glanced down the table. Just like he used to do with his students in high school, Monsieur Gilbert had captured the attention of the tourists. They were feasting on his every word, as well as the meal.

"In order to stay warm and not be buried under the snow," he went on, "I got out every now and then to shovel the snow off my car and around it. After what seemed like countless hours, the storm was over, the sky was blue, and the sun was shining. I packed a few things in my bag and started walking toward the mountain. It took hours before I reached the top, but when I looked down to a valley far below, I could see some trees and four houses beside a river. I hurried down and knocked on the door of the nearest house. A young boy answered and after staring at me, called his father in a surprised voice. The father invited me to come in. The main room was fairly large, with a *charpayee* in each corner."

Before he could go on, several tourists blurted out at the same time, wanting to know what a *charpayee* was.

Monsieur Gilbert smiled and motioned to me, while he took a sip of tea.

I explained that this was a bed made out of wood and rope with a mattress of straw, rushes, or whatever else was available. Charpayees were used as chairs, as well as beds, and could be found in almost every Afghan house.

Monsieur Gilbert acknowledged this with a smile, then continued. "In the center of the room, which served as kitchen, living room and bedroom for the family, was a stove built out of mud with a pipe that went up through the roof. Behind the main room were three smaller rooms-- the young boy's bedroom, one for food storage, and the guest room, which became mine. As I've discovered in other parts of the country, almost all Afghan homes have guest rooms. Even mosques have them.

"After having something to eat, I asked the family about the possibility of getting help to move my car. I was told that no one came here until the spring. Even though I'd lived in Afghanistan for some time and learned a little of the language, I still had problems communicating. But the family made it clear that I was welcome to stay with them until springtime.

"They helped me carry all my belongings in from the car and by this time I was very sweaty and dirty. I asked if I could take a shower and the young boy gave me a bucket of warm water, along with a rusty can, then showed me a little door. Inside was a three-foot square place with wooden walls and a little wooden stand.

"The next day I needed to do some washing and the boy took me to the river. I wasn't sure how to wash my clothes in the icy water. Seeing my ignorance, the boy grabbed a shirt, doused it in the icy water, then put some soap on it. He rubbed the shirt for a while, then started hitting it in a certain way against the rocks on the river bank.

"I nodded and told him, 'I've got it,' then dipped a pair of pants in the river. It was freezing! For every minute that my hands touched the water, I had to put them under my arms for at least fifteen minutes to get them warm again. The young boy was having a wonderful time watching me. Soon he was laughing so hard at my pitiful attempts, that he attracted the attention of some neighbors who joined him for the show.

"In the beginning, I spent most of my time in my room, reading the few books that I had brought under the yellow light of a kerosene lamp. But after a while, I realized if I was going to survive the winter, I had to learn their way of life. I started playing their games and spending more time with the family. The more time I spent with them, the more I liked them, and the more I felt myself becoming part of the family.

"The months went by much quicker than I had thought. Soon I could feel the ground getting softer, see the snow melting and hear birds starting to sing. It was springtime. And time for me to leave.

"On every trip that I've taken away from my own country, I was always happy to return home. But my winter in Jam changed that for me. For the first time, I hated to face so-called civilization and all the problems of city life.

"When it came time to say goodbye, I knew that the family would be insulted if I offered them money, so I left without giving them anything for all their love and hospitality. But I had already decided to come back the next year and bring them a few things to make their lives a little easier. Now, each year I spend my vacation at Jam -- which means The Glass -- and drink my fill of nature's beauty with the people that I love .... "

After hearing Monsieur Gilbert's story, the tourists could hardly wait to visit Jam and Band-e-Amir. But those delights were still a few days down the road.

The following morning, we visited the archeological sites in Bamiyan, including the gigantic Buddhas carved into the mountainside. Originally, the Buddhas' faces had been covered with gold, but when Genghis Khan had ravaged the country, he'd taken the gold and many other precious artifacts.

A door built into one of the toes of the largest Buddha gave us entrance to the mountain. Inside, spiral steps led the way up to different levels where we saw rooms and caves which had been used by monks many centuries before. After climbing over fifty-seven meters, we reached the top of the Buddha's head. Here, we enjoyed a divine view of the city and valley below.

Archeology has always been one of my passions, and before leaving, I stopped to talk with one of the guards who helped take care of the site. He showed me places in the mountainside that had been eroded by heavy rains. Sometimes, he said, the rain washed away parts of the caves, unearthing trinkets and treasures from the ancient city.

To prove his point, he showed me a bracelet that he had found. It was very old, made of heavy silver inlaid with precious stones -- lapis lazuli, garnets and others.

Thinking the bracelet would make a special gift someday for my future wife, I asked the guard if he would be willing to sell it to me and he agreed.

That evening at dinner, I took out the bracelet to show some of the tourists. Sitting beside me was a middle-aged doctor and his wife. Kind and intelligent, I had enjoyed conversing with Henri and his lovely wife from the moment I'd met them. I especially enjoyed hearing their "southern" accent, as they were from Marseilles and the French spoken there sounded much different than that spoken by Parisians.

The doctor and his wife were both impressed with the bracelet's beauty and uniqueness. Henri's wife was especially taken with it and offered to pay me three times what I'd given the guard. I thanked her, but explained that it was a gift for someone and I wasn't interested in selling.

Soon, the bracelet began attracting the attention of the other women on the tour and they were all asking to see it. In the midst of this, I realized there was someone missing from our table. Angelique ... the "angel face."

"She's not feeling well," was Michel's curt answer, when I asked her boyfriend where she was.

Something in his sour expression and the tone of his voice made me suspect they must have had an argument.

"I hate to have her miss dinner," I told him. "Would you mind if I bring her down to dinner?"

He shrugged and said, "I don't care."

Angelique quickly answered my knock, but her obvious surprise when she saw me indicated it was Michel she'd been expecting. I knew from her red, swollen eyes that she must have been crying. but I didn't mention anything about that. Instead, I asked why she hadn't come downstairs to join us for dinner.

"I never want to eat as long as I live!" she answered. "Michel thinks I'm getting too fat and ugly. He thinks there's something wrong with me. No matter what I do or say, it's always wrong. He's the only one who's right. We've had these kind of problems before, but I thought this trip would bring us closer. I was wrong. Tonight, he told me that he doesn't want to be with me any more ... that he wants to be left alone ... Oh, God, I can't believe I'm telling you this!" She turned away and threw herself on the bed. Burying her face in the sheets, she started to sob.

I stood in the doorway, not knowing what to say. Finally, I stepped inside the room and sat down on the edge of the bed.

"Angelique," I said, putting a hand on her back. "If someone tells you that a dog took away your nose, would you check your nose first or run after the dog?"

Beneath my hand, I felt her body shaking, and knew she was laughing and crying at the same time. After a moment, she sat up and wiped her tears with her hand.

"I'm sorry for acting this way," she said, trying to smile. "Michel's right. I'm always doing the wrong thing ...."

"No, he's not!" I grabbed her hand and told her, "You're not fat and ugly! I don't know what his problem is, but look at your beautiful eyes. Any man would love to dream about them every night. Any man would love to wake up in the morning and see your gorgeous face and thank God for having you next to him."

I would have gone on telling Angelique what I thought of her beauty, but the soft touch of her fingers on my mouth suddenly stopped the words.

We sat, staring into each other's eyes, then I said awkwardly, "It's not good for you to miss dinner. Why don't you come downstairs and eat with us?"

Angelique smiled and ran a hand through her long hair. "All right. Just give me a few minutes, and I'll be there."

That night, long after the other tourists had left the dinner table, Angelique and I sat talking together. It was the first time in my life I had ever talked with a young woman other than my sisters. Angelique was couple of years older than I, and was attending college at a French university. We talked about music, books, poetry, and life ... and even when we were silent, it seemed as if our eyes continued the conversation.

It was very late when I walked her to the door of her room.

"*Bonne nuit*," she whispered, touching a palm to my cheek. "And thank you .... "

Impulsively, I took her hand and pressed a kiss into her soft palm. *"Bonne nuit...."*

* * *

Band-e-Amir was just as beautiful as Monsieur Gilbert had described, especially seen in the clear light of early morning. The lake was so calm we could see the whole valley reflected on its surface. I had never seen water so blue.

In Band-e-Amir, the tourists were free to spend the day as they wished, which freed up my time as well. Angelique and I spent the hours riding around the lakes on horseback, eating a picnic lunch, and laughing under the carefree sky of summer.

The next day I was so stiff and sore I could hardly walk, but as tour guide, I tried hard not to show it.

Before leaving Band-e-Amir, I thought it would be wise to call ahead to Jam to check on our reservations. The telephone was an ancient contraption with a hand-crank. After several tries, I finally managed to get through to the owner of the small inn where we were going to stay. I gave him the date and approximate time of our arrival, but when I asked what he was going to prepare for dinner, he told me the inn was very small and they weren't equipped to feed too many people.

"What food do you have?" I yelled into the receiver.

Through the static on the line, his answer came back: "Just some bread, and maybe a little fruit."

I did some quick thinking, and asked him to please bake some bread and kill a lamb for barbequeing, and we would take care of the rest.

Not long after leaving Band-e-Amir, we began passing a lot of nomads on the road. The tourists were fascinated by their life style, and at their request, we made several stops, so they could talk with the nomads and see how they lived.

During one of these stops, I got out of the truck and approached a nomad couple who were sitting by the roadside crying. The mother was holding a young boy of about six or eight on her lap. The child looked very sick and weak, and his only article of clothing was a long, loose shirt. When I asked the mother what the matter was, she lifted up her son's shirt.

The boy's intestines were protruding out of a large opening in his navel and lay across his stomach in a mass of pinkish wet ropes.

I glanced away from the horrible sight to the mother's grief-stricken face and couldn't prevent the tears from running down my own cheeks. Hurrying back to the truck, I found Dr. Henri and asked if he would please look at the boy to see if anything could be done.

I stood beside the boys' parents, while the doctor examined the child. Glancing up at me, Henri shook his head and said quietly, "This boy isn't going to live very long. He needs to be in a hospital."

"There aren't any hospitals for hundreds of miles," I told him. "That's probably why they brought him here. The villagers all know that tours usually have a doctor or nurse along." I looked down at the dying child. "Isn't there anything you can do to help him?"

Henri thoughtfully rubbed his gray mustache with one finger, then got to his feet. "It's going to take a long time because I'm not equipped to handle anything like this -- but I'll do my best."

Remembering my instructions that I was responsible for getting the tour to its destination by nightfall, I returned to the trucks and told the people that the drivers would take them on to the next stop, but Dr. Henri and I were going to stay behind to help this little boy. Some of the tourists agreed with this decision, but others voiced their objections.

Henri walked up as they were arguing back and forth, and said, "I am a doctor, and I believe in God. Maybe this little boy's mother asked God for help, and He chose me to treat him. I will never be able to live with myself if I don't do what I can for him."

That beautiful speech changed everyone's mind, and from that moment on, all the tourists were united in their decision to stay.

The doctor got his few medical supplies and we carried the boy to his parents' tent. It took nearly seven hours to perform the surgery. When he was finished, he put an *afghani* coin about two inches in diameter on top of the gauze bandage which protected the boy's navel. Then he wrapped the remaining gauze tightly around the child's abdomen.

Dr. Henri looked up at me with a broad smile. "Tell the boy never to spend this coin, because it just might be the one that saved his life."

I was smiling myself as I translated the good news for the anxious parents.

The father was so happy and grateful, he grabbed the doctor's hands and kissed them again and again. And this time, the mother's tears came from joy.

When Dr. Henri and I returned to the trucks, the tourists cheered and applauded. Looking at their faces, I knew that no one would ever forget the day that a roadside stop turned the Central Road of Afghanistan into an invisible hospital for some poor villagers.

The next day's journey was the most difficult of the entire trip. The sun was hot, the roads were dusty and rough, and we had to travel through several high mountain passes. Several times I would take pitchers of water from the barrels and pour it over the tourists to help cool them off. Two minutes later, they were dry.

A few miles from Jam, there were no roads at all and the trucks had to drive through the shallow waters of a river.

I glanced out the window, thinking this must be the same river where Monsieur Gilbert had washed his clothes on that cold winter day. Now these high mountain valleys wore the green dress of summer and there were fruit trees growing on the river bank. The trees were so close we could reach out and pick luscious ripe apricots to eat on our way.

Then we left the trees behind to climb even higher, the trucks following a narrow track between the steep, rocky sides of the mountains. After making a sharp turn around the cliff, we were rewarded with a breathtaking view of our destination. Straight ahead were the rushing waters of a two mountain rivers, and some twenty yards further, the beautiful minarette of Jam which had stood proudly over the centuries, protected by the lofty Hindu-Kush mountains.

Soon after our arrival, preparations were underway for the barbeque. While the lamb was cooking, we built a big bonfire in a beautiful meadow near the inn. No one was cold, as the evening air was pleasantly cool after the day's blistering heat, but the site was perfect for a crackling fire and the warm commaraderie it invited.

After dinner, under the light of the stars and the moon, with the beautiful music of the river to play for us, everyone began dancing and singing. I glanced around the happy crowd, and noticed Dr. Henri and his wife sitting on a wooden bench near the fire. Seeing the doctor's kindly features softened by the glow of firelight, my thoughts returned to his unselfish act the day before. I remembered his words to the tourists ... "Maybe this little boy's mother asked God for help, and he chose me to treat him. I'll never be able to live with myself if I don't do what I can."

Tears filled my eyes as I walked toward the doctor and his wife. I hoped the darkness would hide the sight of them, but I knew it couldn't hide my trembling, emotional voice.

"When your husband operated on that little boy, he gave my people a gift that I will never forget," I told her. "Now I want to give you something in return ...." Taking the silver bracelet from my pocket, I put it in her hand.

For a moment, all she could do was stare at the bracelet. Then she jumped up and threw her arms around me. Dr. Henri looked at me with his kind smile, and I could see the glow of the fire in the happy shine of his tears.

Our last major stop was Herat, Afghanistan's second largest city. Here, the tour had reservations in a modern hotel that had a large swimming pool and beautiful rooms for its guests.

I was given a very nice room as well, but I had somewhere else in mind to sleep that night. Since childhood, I have loved sleeping outside under the light of the stars. Just outside the hotel was a large garden with several trees and a small stream running through it. I put a *charpayee* near the stream and made my bed for the night.

I wanted to spend a few minutes enjoying my peaceful surroundings and the star-filled sky, but we had traveled a long distance that day and sleep came quickly. Sometime later, I felt a hand covering my mouth. I woke up angrily, then I heard a soft voice saying, "Shhh, it's me-- Angelique."

At first, I thought I was dreaming, but when she touched my lips briefly with hers, I knew it was real. Lying down beside me, she put her head on my chest and began whispering her thoughts and emotions. Angelique's beautiful voice, accompanied by the chant of the running water and the cries of the leaves resisting the advances of the wind, was like a song pampering all my senses. When she raised her head and started kissing my neck, her silky hair brushed against my face. Soon, I felt the heat of her irresistible breasts getting closer to my thirsty lips, and the aura of her soft body next to my skin. Like a hungry infant who has just found the source of milk for the first time, I pressed my lips against her mouth, her cheeks, her eyes and her naked shoulders.

    No one had ever described to me that there was so much burning and melting joy to be found in the arms of a woman. No one had ever told me that the closeness between male and female would have such an impact over every nerve of my body. I felt like an inexperienced swimmer who was riding the wildest waves in the ocean of desire. With every kiss, I was more addicted to the pleasures her existance could offer. With Angelique in my arms, everything around me seemed more wonderful. The stars looked brighter, the moon bigger and more perfect. The perfume of the trees and the flowers was sweeter.

    I didn't realize the night was getting shorter until I heard the song of the birds praising the sunrise and felt the cold breeze of dawn kissing my face. When Angelique left my bed, I lay thinking about the memories of the night just past, amazed at all we had shared and grateful that she was going to spend one more week in my country.

    When I returned home after the tour, my family was surprised to see me looking so happy and healthy. After a few hours of talking, they discovered the source of my happiness. Angelique. My sisters couldn't wait to meet her. I told them that I was going to bring her over the following day for dinner.

Where the night I spent with Angelique had passed far too quickly, the night before I would see her again seemed to drag on forever. I lay awake for hours, planning out all the places I wanted to take her. Anticipation and excitement woke me well before dawn. I sat by my window, watching the vague silhouettes of the mountains and waiting for the sun's magical fingers to bring those silhouettes to life.

At last it was time for me to pick Angelique up from her hotel. As soon as she saw me, my "angel face" opened her arms and held me tightly. Then she laughed and said, "I'm ready. Let's go see your town!"

It was my town. My favorite city in the whole world. I took her to different bazaars and she was excited to see me bargain with the sellers over prices. I showed her the museum, the historical places, the parks, my favorite restaurants, even the school I used to attend.

That evening when we arrived at my home for dinner, my family was waiting in the courtyard to greet our guest. My sisters spoke a little French, and Mina insisted on taking Angelique to her room. After what seemed like a long time, but was probably no more than a few minutes, Mina asked me to join them. I walked in the room and saw Angelique wearing Mina's favorite black Afghan dress with gold embroidery.

"Mina offered me this dress as a present," she said with an excited smile. "Isn't that nice?"

She looked so beautiful and so Afghan in that dress that I couldn't find the words to tell her. For the few hours she spent in our home, Angelique was the center of our attention and made a place for herself in the hearts of everyone.

The next day I packed a picnic lunch for the two of us and took Angelique to my childhood hideaway -- a special spot on the summit of the mountain not far from my home.

In this high place I could look over the city of Kabul and watch the birds flying beneath me. It was a place where the friendly rocks understood the language of my emotions whenever I was sad or angry. A place where I could listen to the praises of the water as it ripped through the heart of the rocks on its way to nourish the chapped lips of the land below. For years, I had come here alone whenever I needed solitude and space. Now my need in coming was not for solitude, but the desire to share its wonder and hidden meanings with someone I loved.

The morning of her departure, I told myself I didn't have the courage to get up and take Angelique to the airport, but I did it anyway. Inside the cab, neither of us said much. I think we both knew that as soon we opened our mouths, our tears would do the talking in front of the driver.

A last kiss. Tears. Promises. A few choked words of farewell. Then she was gone. I waited and watched until I saw her plane disappearing into the clouds of memories.

After Angelique left, I began going to my favorite hideaway more often. I found myself touching and talking to the rock she sat upon. I thought of every little thing she said and did -- the way she smiled, the way she talked, and the way she moved her hair away from her face.

A week later, I received a ten-page letter. The writing was small, feminine and very neat, with the exception of some blurred ink spots which I thought may have been caused by the precious drops of her tears. The last page was full of red lip prints, made by the perfect shape of her mouth. God knows how many times I kissed those paper lips before I went to bed, wishing that I could dream of her again and again.

For a few months, our correspondence continued with passionate fervor and poetry took on a new, deeper meaning for me. Then, after six months or so, Angelique's letters became shorter and the distance between them much longer.

Thinking of her, the lines of a poem began to haunt me with their painful truth as well as their beauty.

Whenever the perfume of your closeness
    surrounds the sky of my solitude,
I think of the lonely spring that I'm going to spend
    without being in your arms.
The joy of my memories are like the shadows of my
    love;
The closer I look at them, the faster they disappear ....

I never saw or heard from my "angel face" again.

Chapter 12

AFTER AHMAD'S ARREST that August afternoon, his family waited anxiously for news of his condition or whereabouts. None came. During the weeks which followed, soldiers and members of KhAD returned to the Sharifi home again and again. Each time they searched, terrorized and destroyed the family's belongings as well as their fragile hopes.

Soon after his escape from *Sedarat*, Farid had gone into hiding. He and Mina and their infant daughter moved from place to place, living with friends and members of the resistance for a few days at a time, in an effort to keep one step ahead of the secret police. Occasionally, Mina managed a brief visit with her family, by disguising herself in a *chadiri*, the enveloping, head-to-foot veil still worn by some Afghan women. But those visits were few and far between.

The threat of arrest kept most of Ahmad's friends far away as well. Only Samad and Zia still visited the family. Samad was especially faithful. Every week he came by without fail, hoping for news of his friend. And every week the answer was the same. But that didn't stop him. Not coming would be like an admission that Ahmad was dead, and Samad refused to believe this was so.

The agony of not knowing whether Ahmad was alive or dead once prompted Mina to risk a visit to the Office of the Interior, where a partial list of those who had been executed had been posted. Mina had read only a few names, before dread and anxiety over the possibility of seeing her brother's name caused her to fall over in a dead faint.

By September of '79, it was estimated that more than 17,000 Afghans had been executed as a result of Taraki's and Amin's repressive regime, and some 30,000 others were still in prison. Members of the Afghan army were deserting in droves to join the ranks of the *mujahidin.* Civil servants, university professors, doctors, students and other members of the educated elite, continued to disappear from their places of work, their homes and the bazaars. As the death toll mounted, waves of people began fleeing Afghanistan's borders into neighboring Pakistan and Iran.

Members of the Sharifi family were included in that frightened migration of souls. After a quiet wedding, Ahmad's sister Rahella and her new husband Anwar, left Afghanistan for the comparative safety of Iran where he would practice medicine.

The large house on a hillside overlooking Kabul seemed strangely empty and silent in spite of the family members still living there.

Ahmad's mother kept up the necessary chores of running a household, but her son's absence was like an open wound that never healed. The pain of going into his room, seeing his French books and cassette tapes lying on the shelves, never lessened. In spite of the fact there were still others to care for, without Ahmad's vital loving presence, it seemed as if all the music and laughter were gone ....

Throughout the weeks of uncertainty and emotional upheaval, Latif faithfully attended to his daily prayers -- but that didn't stop him from wondering why. Why these violent threats and attacks on his family? Who would be next? Zoor? Habib? Surely not Rahim, who was only a boy.

His oldest son Habib drove a cab in the city, and it seemed that every day he brought news of more arrests and more violence. Such things were completely alien to Latif's gentle nature. For the sake of the family, as well as his own sanity, Latif tried to keep busy -- his clever hands were always finding something to build or repair -- but pain and loss had etched new lines deep into his features. His children were his life, and now, one by one, they were being torn away from him.

* * *

Outside the walls of *Sedarat*, life went on despite political upheavals in the government. Across the way, tourists and vendors still bartered over goods on Kabul's famous Chicken Street, while young people walked the paths of Zarnegar Park and attended classes at the French High School, *Istqlal*. Stores dealing in sales of rugs, fur and leather still opened their doors for business across the street from *Sedarat's* iron gates. And in embassies and offices around the corner from those concealing walls, ambassadors and envoys continued to meet and express properly worded concern over the country's difficulties.

Within those high walls, Ahmad and hundreds of nameless others like him, struggled to survive the endless days and nights. Each day scores of new prisoners arrived to undergo their tutoring in torture. The lessons were learned quickly and most inmates stayed only a week or two, at which time they were either transferred to the main prison or received a release at the hands of death.

For those inmates granted the privilege of enduring another day, there was a monthly variation in the routine called the "Inspection of Prisoners." During this event, inmates were ordered to line up in one of the yards, after which, each man would step forward, give his name, how many days he had been imprisoned, then state his crime against the government.

Ahmad's reputation grew among prisoners and guards alike, not only because of the unusual length of his imprisonment, but the uniqueness of his crime. Simply stated, it was: "I am Farid's brother-in-law."

Farid's brother-in-law was both a puzzle and a threat to the officials at *Sedarat*. For months, they had hesitated killing the young man on the offchance he might be withholding a scrap of vital information about Farid or his friends. Now, it seemed highly unlikely this was so. Despite his innocence, *Sedarat's* longest resident had far too much knowledge of the atrocities committed there to ever be released.

Ahmad knew every guard and Investigator by name and reputation, including Asidullah Sarwari, the infamous head of KhAD whose size and cruelty had earned him the nicknames of "King Kong" and "the butcher." It was Sarwari who had overseen his torture and interrogation that first week. In the ensuing months, Ahmad frequently saw the huge man in prison halls and offices.

Equally as dangerous as being able to identify the prison personnel, Ahmad was eyewitness to much of the corruption going on within the Ministry of Justice. He knew for example, that in addition to their regular salaries, Investigators were paid 500 *afghanis* for each "confession" they were able to obtain. This monetary incentive greatly increased the Investigators' creativity in devising new torture methods for their victims.

And there was more. Trucks arrived weekly at the prison, filled with the confiscated possessions of those who had been arrested. Ahmad had helped unload the trucks many times, and was appalled by all the television sets and furniture, the bedding, clothes, watches and other personal belongings that had been stolen by the government. The booty was divided among members of KhAD and other officials at *Sedarat.*

Whenever Ahmad saw an Investigator wearing a new suit or a pair of shiny new shoes, he couldn't help wondering about the former owners and their supposed crimes against the government.

Of all the prison personnel, there was only one for whom Ahmad had any respect. The guard, Ahmad Shah. From his observations, the young man seemed intelligent, educated and totally lacking in the cruel characteristics of his co-workers. Ever since his experience with the French couple, and the morning that Ahmad Shah had brought him his bread, a mutual respect and friendship had sprung up between the two young men. Unspoken and never too overt, it existed nonetheless.

Ahmad's friendship with the guard also made him privy to occasional outside news. From him, Ahmad learned that Prime Minister Amin's nephew and son-in-law had replaced the hated Sarwari as head of KhAD. Asidullah Amin was a slender, younger version of his famous uncle, but his innocuous appearance masked a streak of cruelty and cunning that quickly earned him a reputation nearly as feared as that of his predecessor, "King Kong."

Other dramatic changes had taken place that autumn, most of which were completely unknown to the inmates of *Sedarat*. President Taraki was gone and Prime Minister Amin had appointed himself as the country's new president. Rumors were flying about the real cause of Taraki's sudden demise. Informed sources privately agreed that the powerful prime minister had had Taraki under his control for months. This made Moscow very uneasy, as Hafizullah Amin was not only a dozen years younger and more charismatic than Taraki, he was also more difficult to control.

In early September, a healthy, smiling Taraki had flown to Havana, Cuba, for some "diplomatic" meetings with Fidel Castro. While there, Taraki received private communication from his loyal "hit man" Sarwari, that Amin intended to kill him. Taraki, with encouragement from Moscow, decided to turn the tables and eliminate Amin instead.

Accordingly, Sarwari arranged to have his men assassinate the prime minister on his way to the Kabul airport to welcome Taraki back from Havana. What Sarwari didn't know was that Amin had been informed of the plot by his own spy, Major Taroon, a police commandant in Taraki's entourage. Fully warned, Amin replaced Sarwari's men with loyal army units as his escort to the airport.

On September 11, a smiling Taraki flew back to Kabul fully expecting that his "loyal student," Amin had been eliminated. Taraki's surprise at being greeted by a smiling prime minister who was very much alive was obvious. For the benefit of the press and those present, both men engaged in a comradely bear hug.

The Kabuli populace had no idea of the subversive plots, subplots and treachery that were going on between their president and his prime minister. Those listening to Radio Kabul that warm September day heard Taraki's reception described in glowing terms:

"The great leader of the people of Afghanistan, Nur Mohammad Taraki, today returned to his beloved country and was warmly and unprecedentedly received by tens of thousands of our noble and patriotic people, carrying flowers and revolutionary slogans ... After the airport ceremonies, our great leader was escorted by Hafizullah Amin ... his faithful student and the great commander of the Great Saur Revolution, up to the side of his special car .... He was given a rousing and tumultuous welcome by thousands of patriotic citizens who were carrying thousands of pictures of the great leader of the people .... They were shouting slogans of: 'Good health to Comrade Taraki!'

Three days later, Taraki disappeared, the thousands of pictures of him were taken down and his health was rumored to be not good at all.

On September 14, Hafizullah Amin fired the top four members of Taraki's cabinet, including the infamous Sarwari. Furious, but still smiling, Taraki telephoned the prime minister that same day and invited him to the People's Palace to talk things over. Suspecting a plot, Amin at first refused, but finally agreed after the Soviet Ambassador, Alexander Puzanov, assured him there was nothing to worry about and personally guaranteed his safety.

Ever cautious, Amin brought along an armed escort, just in case. When he arrived at the palace, there was no time for talking. Instead, a "wild West" type shootout occurred in which several people were killed. Among the casualties was Amin's supporter and spy, Major Taroon, who was standing in front of the Prime Minister when the first shots were fired.

Amin escaped from the fracus unhurt, and returned later that afternoon with some of his supporters to take Taraki prisoner.

The following day, Radio Kabul announced that the president had resigned from office because of "health reasons." Not long after this, Prime Minister Amin confirmed the fact by stating that Taraki was "definitely sick."

Nothing more was heard about the ailing former president until October 10, when the *Kabul Times* printed a small back page announcement stating simply: "Nur Mohammad Taraki died yesterday morning as a result of a serious illness which he had been suffering for some time."

The real illness, according to informed sources was a lack of oxygen brought on by three members of the presidential guard who had smothered Taraki with a pillow.

Prime Minister Amin smilingly stepped in to take over the government, pledging to the people in a dramatic speech, that under his leadership conditions would improve throughout the country. Among other things, Amin promised that "nobody would be sent to prison without being charged with an offense," and "Furthermore, whoever may have been arrested without due cause will be released immediately. There will not be any type of pressure or force used on any individual to make him act contrary to his sacred religious beliefs."

Through Amin's slogan of "security, legality and justice," everyone in Afghanistan was promised "full liberties and inviolable democratic rights."

Most Afghans knew only too well that Hafizullah Amin was one of the main reasons why security, legality and justice did not exist in their country. In fact, the new president's policies sounded a bit ridiculous, since he was saying in effect, that the government would stop doing the terrible things it had been doing under his leadership all along.

As for the promised changes, Ahmad and thousands of other political prisoners were silent witnesses that President Amin could not be trusted. For every prisoner released, scores of others were arrested and imprisoned without trial.

An American diplomat described the mood in Kabul that autumn in chilling terms: "There is an atmosphere of mortal fear and dread pervading the country, as virtually every Afghan ... wonders if tonight is his night to fall into the clutches of the security authorities, perhaps to disappear into one of the country's overcrowded prisons, never to be heard from again...."

Chapter 13

THROUGHOUT OUR DAYS and nights in *Sedarat*, my fellow prisoners and I often found consolation and strength in sharing our individual stories of arrest and torture. Some of the men had been arrested because of their affiliation with the *mujahidin* and other resistance groups. Others had been taken because they belonged to the opposition party. But there were numerous inmates whose so-called crimes were not so dramatic. I always felt sorry for the poor store owner who was arrested because he refused to sell eggs at a discounted price to a Communist party member.

In spite of our circumstances, hope was something we all tried to keep alive, no matter how small the spark, even though each of us knew the time might come when we would hear our names called at that deadly hour of night.

One man, who had been a teacher, told me candidly, "I know they're going to kill me no matter what, because I told them everything I knew. I also made up a lot of stories to end my suffering because I couldn't handle it. My torture began with lots of beating, then electrical shocks. After that they put me in a dark room for days. The room was full of lice and fleas and other kinds of bugs. Since my hands and legs were tied behind me, the bugs were no different than the Investigators in sucking my blood and torturing me. That's how I lost all my eyelashes, because the bugs were running all over my face. In the beginning, I was fighting -- fighting the bugs by rubbing my face against anything I could find. My skin got so thin from all the rubbing that it was bleeding everywhere. This gave the bugs an even better opportunity to win the competition of torture. But the Investigators didn't give up. They kept me hungry and thirsty for two days. Then one of them came in and released my hands and legs. He even apologized for the way I had been treated. I couldn't believe the sudden change. The Investigator brought two big watermelons into the room, then left. I was so hungry and thirsty I ate both of them as fast as I could.

"A few minutes later, the Investigator returned with two soldiers and a chair. They took my clothes off, sat me on the chair and started wrapping a long rope all around me. Then, with some tape and thread, they tied my penis so tight that I couldn't go to the bathroom.

"In those worst hours of my life, I was screaming, crying, swearing, begging, praying. Nothing worked. I thought my body was going to explode. Finally, the Investigator came back and started his questions all over again. This time, I told him exactly what he wanted to hear."

After listening to this experience, another prisoner spoke up and said, "You won't believe my story. They have these kind of torture places all over the country. I was in another state when the secret police arrested me at a relative's home and took me to prison. Another of my relatives happened to work at the prison, but the Investigators didn't know that. My relative found out the times when I was going to be tortured, and right before the scheduled time, he would come to my room and give me different kinds of drugs, so I wouldn't feel the torture. I could still feel the electrical shocks, but I had no pain.

"After trying for days, the Investigators gave my case to a very sharp and cruel man. He tied me onto a chair and said, 'You think you're tough. You're going to speak like a bird.'

"As he was wrapping the electrical wires around my toes, I started giggling and trying to get my legs and feet away. He realized by my actions that I was ticklish, so he threw away the wires and started tickling me instead. Soon, I had three people tickling me for hours until I passed out. After a while, I was getting so sensitive to this, that all I had to do was see their hands coming toward me, and I would faint from laughing. The Investigator was right. After a few days, I was talking like a bird ....."

Unlike most of the inmates, there were a few, who for one reason or another were given special privileges. One of these was a man we called, "Engineer," who ran the cantina. Because of his connection with some powerful people in the prison, Engineer was given his own room. He even shaved and combed his hair every day, and had other luxuries that none of the other inmates enjoyed. Books, for example. Engineer was interested in world history and Freudian psychology, and had several texts on these subjects.

He offered me a job on Fridays, selling fresh apple and carrot juice to soldiers, Investigators, and those inmates who had money to buy some. Engineer supplied me with a juice extractor and the necessary ingredients. For wages, I was given a pack of cigarettes at the end of the day. I tried to make that one pack last until the next week, but most of the time, the cigarettes were gone long before then, because I shared them with other prisoners, especially a young mechanic named Jan Mohammed who had done the same for me until his money ran out.

On Fridays, while I stood in front of the cantina waiting for customers, Engineer was usually stretched out in a comfortable chair reading. History had been one of my favorite subjects in school, and I always asked him to please read outloud. Listening to the accounts of various wars, battles and other events in world history, I found myself thinking how unfortunate it was that most of what we knew of the past should be written from the viewpoint of the conquerors. What about all the nameless others who lived and died over the centuries? Surely their lives were just as important to God as the lives of mighty generals and kings. It seemed very wrong to me that they should be forgotten.

I was discussing these ideas and feelings with my fellow inmates one evening, when someone said, "Whoever gets out of here alive needs to write about what happened here, so the world won't forget about us and all those who died."

The others in our little circle were in complete agreement with this. What we didn't know was if any of us would ever leave *Sedarat* alive.

* * *

Many times during my adventure at *Sedarat* -- especially when I woke up in the middle of the night -- having nothing else to do, I would sit on my so-called bed and observe my fellow inmates in various sleeping positions. In spite of the similarities that we as human beings share with one another, there are still some special characteristics that make each of us unique. Not only in our appearance, but also our habits and reactions. With so many people crammed together in one small room, sleeping conditions were often humorous, as well as pathetic.

Those men sleeping closest to the walls had no space to stretch out their legs, so they would try to maintain them at a 90 degree angle, with their behinds resting against the cool walls. Very often, while they were sleeping, the men's legs would fall down on either side, and sometimes they even crashed into another man's face. Some inmates tried to sleep with their legs hunched up against their stomachs, which gave them an awkward, yet amusing appearance -- especially those who were wearing baggy Afghan pants that would fall down, exposing their naked hairy legs sticking up in the air.

Depending on the number of occupants in the room, very often there were men who ended up sleeping face to face. If one of them had a beard or a mustache, it would brush against the other man's nose no matter how hard he tried to avoid it. I had to smile, thinking about the rude shock those two would have when they opened their eyes in the morning and discovered how they had spent the night.

And then, God bless their souls, there were those snoring little monsters. When they breathed in, it sounded like the music of a clogged flute filled with water. When they breathed out, watch for the trains!

In spite of these humorous situations, I couldn't help feeling there was something innocent, almost sacred about people when they were asleep. Seeing their diverse physical make-up, and receiving the energy of their auras, I was filled with a loving fascination for being part of humanity, and also an immense admiration for God's creation of two worlds beneath one small roof: The physical world where He allowed us the patience and capabilities to accept our destiny; and the precious world of sleep when our bodies rested, and our minds and spirits traveled beyond time and space.

Sleep was the amazing vehicle which could transport us to a twilight of comfort and love, like the arms of our mothers; other times, we might visit a kingdom of peace and calm, like the tranquility found in the mountains. We all longed for this hazy heaven of dreams where the queen of our wishful desires granted us the magical honey of her lips. But before reaching this heavenly ground, we had to confront some unpleasant elements of competition. Besides the 'music of the flute' and the 'siren of the train', there were other distractions ... blood-sucking lice and mosquitoes, the persistent flies, the cries and moaning of the injured ... the heat, and the cold. And worst of all, there was the voice of the devil who came to wake us in the morning, and the shouts of the soldier who read his master's decisions late at night.

On one of those numberless nights, I heard heavy footsteps approaching our room. Moments later, the door opened and a soldier stepped inside, commanding us with sneering irony to: "Get up! Make room for one more of your brothers."

In a matter of seconds, everyone was on their feet. Even though the chamber of doom was already packed, we all tried to squeeze a little more. In the dim light of one yellowish bulb, I saw the face of a giant, bending down so he could get through the door.

Without being asked, everyone tightened a few more notches in order to shorten the chain of human links and make room for this new member.

The giant entered, and when he stretched out his arms to remove his jacket, it seemed as if half the room was suddenly in shadow. The newcomer stood well over six feet, and had very broad shoulders. Adding a few more inches to his impressive height was a Russian hat, which I knew would make him the object of the men's jokes, as anything that came from Russia had the effect of cayenne pepper sprinkled on the veins of hate.

"I wonder how they're going to hold him down for torturing," Noor commented quietly. "And the small portion of food that we receive will probably vanish between his teeth before it ever touches his stomach."

I smiled at him. "I don't think the soldiers in charge of food will want this guy hungry and mad at the same time."

Waking up many times during the night was routine for us. That first night, every time I turned to look at him, the giant was awake. Early the next morning, before the pilgrimage of the guard Awaz's shiny nose, one of the inmates commented to our new guest, "You didn't sleep last night."

The giant spoke for the first time. "No. I have problems with my stomach. It's either an ulcer or too much acid. When the soldiers took me, I didn't have a chance to think about my medicine. And when I'm upset, it gets worse."

Listening to his deep voice and the way he spoke, I had the impression that he must be an educated individual.

"I think carrots are good for stomach problems," one of the men suggested.

The giant's broad shoulders slumped. "Where am I going to find carrots in here?" he mumbled.

For one whole week, the giant wasn't taken for interrogation, which made the rest of us very suspicious that he might be an informer.

Informer or not, I couldn't help feeling sorry for him, and when I went to work at the cantina that Friday, I managed to hide a few carrots in my pockets to bring back to the giant for his stomach troubles.

A few days later when we returned from work, he was gone. We didn't see or hear from him for four days, and everyone was sure he was one of them.

On the fourth night the soldiers brought him back to our room. The man's entire body was shaking, and we could see he'd been badly beaten. His sad expression and the circles of fear around his eyes, gave him the haunted look of a child who had been emotionally and physically abused. He certainly didn't look like the giant who had joined us a week and a half earlier.

We all felt very guilty for our suspicions and did our best to help him. And when Friday came, I stole a few more carrots to give to him.

One of the things I remember him telling us was, "I can handle the beatings and the electricity, but I will never forget the humiliation. I'm a professor of philosophy, and I have hundreds of students their age. I couldn't believe the things they were doing to me ...."

From then on, we called him *Ustad* -- the teacher. As time, the healer of all wounds went by, Ustad began teaching us about literature, history, and philosophy from the time of ancient Greece to the latest ideas of Jean Paul Sartre, and existentialism.

One night, the soldiers took our teacher away for more questioning and we never saw him again. Although Ustad was gone, the vibration of his deep voice and the things he taught us remained, stimulating the cells of knowledge in our minds.

For me, *zardac* (meaning carrots), the golden fruit of Afghanistan will always carry sweet memories of Ustad, whose real name we never knew, and the juicy sensation of the theft I never felt guilty about. Instead, I was left to wonder why they kept picking out, one by one, the best flowers and the pride of the garden of knowledge and human qualities that shined in the darkness of our room.

Chapter 14

THE HOLY MONTH of Ramazan is a special time when, from dawn to dusk, Moslems are not supposed to eat, drink, smoke, swear, or even have bad thoughts. In spite of the difficult conditions in *Sedarat*, most of the inmates diligently tried to observe these rules.

Ramazan was even more special for us that year, because it was during this time that the soldiers brought Kojah to our room. An older man, standing barely 5'2" tall, Kojah had a long pointy nose which perfectly suited his bearded face. His curly hair reminded me of rice and black beans, since the original dark color was now peppered with gray.

The first day Kojah arrived, he was dressed in a beautiful suit and looked very distinguished. In talking with him, we learned that he was accused of supplying weapons to the rebels. We learned, too, that Kojah was a very rich man and the owner of a large company. But it wasn't his money that impressed us. Kojah was a storyteller.

The old man had a God-given talent and such eloquence, that when he was telling a story, he immediately captured our attention. It was as if we were living his stories and the slaves of his imagination. For a week following his arrival, Kojah's name was not called for torture and we had the privilege and pleasure of listening to his wonderful fairy tales each night after dinner.

Before the pleasure could begin, we first had to endure the pain. About a half hour before dusk, Awaz's gruff voice would order us to leave work and get in line. With baton in hand and crude insults running from his mouth like filth in a sewer, the tall, skinny guard brought us back to the courtyard where we had a short time to wash up before going to our rooms.

The washing facilities were primitive at best, but with a little ingenuity and cooperation, we managed to rinse off some of the day's grime. The prison yard was littered with broken pieces of clay pots. One inmate would get the hose and start filling up the pieces with water, while the rest of us paired up to pour water on each other's hands. Since there were no towels, we used our clothes to dry ourselves.

After dinner, we would lie down and ask like a group of eager children, "Kojah, tell us a story."

Listening to him, those eternal nights were too short for the wonderful tales that stimulated and expanded our frozen imaginations. For Kojah, telling stories was not only an escape, it was his passion. We could feel that passion in the rich tone of his voice and when the story was a sad one, we could even see the tears in his eyes.

I asked him once how he knew so many beautiful fairy tales. "I have ten grandchildren," he answered with a wistful smile. "Each time they come to my house, they want to hear a new story. Some of the tales were passed down to me from my father and his father, but others -- like the saying goes, 'the need is the father of creating' -- I made up for my grandchildren."

There is an old saying: "In the city of the blind, a one-eyed man is king."

Kojah was our king.

We all wanted to see beyond the obstacles and walls of our prison. The old man's fairy tales gave us the wings to fly and the beautiful mirage of freedom. It wasn't as if we had no imagination or power of mind ourselves, but compared to Kojah, the rest of us were like a bird with wet wings.

On one of those memorable evenings, the old man sat cross-legged before us. "*Bood nabood* ...." he began, which means, 'There was and there wasn't.' "Tonight, I'm going to tell you the story of *Ghezal e Baharistan* --- the Gazelle of the Spring Land .... A long time ago, I mean centuries ago, in God's most favorite planet, the planet where love is the seed and beauty is the fruit of everything one's eyes can see and one's heart can feel -- there was a place called Baharistan ... the land of the spring.

"No one knew or appreciated the beauty of this place more than a man by the name of Amir. Amir made his living selling wood and the fruit that he picked from the forests in the mountains. He had five children, all of them sons. His wife, whom he loved dearly, died giving birth to their last child. Unlike the first four brothers, the youngest son was born bald and ugly.

"Amir didn't like this son because he blamed the child for his wife's death. He was so bitter, he didn't even bother to give the baby a name. Not long after the birth of this son, Amir noticed an amazing phenomenon. Every time he went to the forest, a little gazelle followed him about, staring at him with tearful eyes. It was as if the animal were trying to give him a message. The more Amir looked at the gazelle, the more certain he became that there was something familiar about it. Then he realized the gazelle's eyes reminded him of his wife's eyes.

"When Amir came home from the forest, he took his infant son in his arms for the first time and gave him the name of Ghezal. From then on, the boy was raised as a normal child. As Ghezal grew older, he became as strong as his older brothers, but he was still plain in appearance. Ghezal was the only one willing to help his father with his work, so Amir taught the boy everything he knew.

"One day while father and son were working, Amir, who had a heavy load of wood on his back, fell off a cliff into the river below. Ghezal pulled his father out of the water onto the river bank, and realized with anguish that the person he loved so much was dying.

"Even though he was too badly injured to talk, Amir wanted to teach his son one last lesson. With his left hand, he took a green leaf from the river bank. With his right hand, he tried to reach under the flowing water. Then he dropped the leaf in the water and weakly pointed for Ghezal to watch as it floated on the surface.

"Ghezal glanced from the leaf to his dying father, too distraught to understand what the man was trying to tell him.

"After the funeral, Ghezal came to the river every day, hoping to understand what it was his father wanted to tell him."

Kojah paused in his storytelling to glance around the room. "What do you think the fable means?" he asked us.

Some inmates answered that by getting the green leaf and touching the water, Amir wanted to tell his son to become a farmer and grow things. Others thought the green leaf symbolized treasure, and perhaps Amir had some kind of treasure buried under the water.

"You all have good answers," Kojah said, "but listen to the story and you'll find out." The old man took a deep breath, his bushy brows lifted, and the richness of his wonderful voice carried us away once more.

"Since Ghezal was unable to figure out the meaning of his father's last message, he went to see an old man called Hakeem, who had had many experiences in his life, and to whom people often went for advice. After listening to the young man, Hakeem said he wanted to think about the puzzle for a few days before answering. Two days later, the old man summoned Ghezal. 'Your father was a very wise man,' he said. 'He wanted to tell you the greatest secret of life. Now listen carefully. Water is life. Your father was searching for the fish under the water. When you watch fish swimming, they are always happy and free. The green leaf symbolizes prosperity, or treasure. And the real treasure in life is goodness. What your father meant by these two things, was that goodness and happiness go hand in hand. By tossing the leaf onto the surface of the water, Amir was showing you that no matter where you throw goodness, it will never sink. It will always be there, shining on the surface. And when you look under the leaf, just below the surface, what do you see? The fish again -- happy and free.'

"Ghezal thanked the old man and promised himself that he was going to live the rest of his life according to this last message from his father.

"Now the ruler of the land of Beharistan was a man by the name of Jaber. Jaber became king by the power of black magic and sorcery. He was very famous for his cruelty and loved only two things in life. Power and his only daughter, the Princess Henah.

When the princess reached a marriageable age, King Jaber decided that he would only give her hand to the man who had more power than himself. To prove himself, the suitor would have to meet and pass three conditions. Many strong young men, including Ghezal's four older brothers tried for the princess's hand, but none of them were able to pass even the first condition. After his last brother failed and was banished, Ghezal decided he would also try for the princess' hand.

"Before going to meet the king, Ghezal went down to the river one last time and sat on a rock, looking at the place where he last saw his father alive. Suddenly, he noticed a bottle floating on the surface of the water. Ghezal plucked the bottle from the river and discovered a strange creature inside -- a tiny man who begged him to open the lid.

Curious, Ghezal decided to remove the lid and swirling clouds of vapor rushed from the bottle. As the vapor surrounded him in a colorful mist, Ghezal heard a deep voice saying, 'Don't be afraid. I won't harm you. You have just saved my existence. Otherwise, I would have been doomed to remain inside that bottle for eternity.'

"'Who are you?" Ghezal asked in a trembling voice. 'And what were you doing in the bottle?'

"'I cannot tell you my name or show you my face,' the voice answered, 'but once I was human just like you. Only I was so greedy and power-hungry that I sold my heart and my soul to the devil. I thought then that I had everything I was looking for, but now I know I was wrong. You don't realize how fortunate you are. You can bring beauty wherever you go just by working hard. You can enjoy the fruits of the blisters in your hands. There is comfort in your sadness. There is joy in your loneliness. Try to imagine not being able to laugh, cry, or feel emotion. More than anything else, I want to become human again. My only chance to do this is by serving someone in great need. You can give me this opportunity by allowing me to help you when you need it most. Here are some strands of my hair. When you want me, burn this and I'll be there. But remember, I can only help you once.'

"'I don't know whether I'll be alive to use this,' Ghezal told the voice, 'because tomorrow I am going to try to pass the first condition of King Jaber.'

'King Jaber!' the voice boomed, and the veils of vapor trembled around Ghezal. 'He is the cause of my problems, too. But don't be afraid of him. You already possess the necessary weapons for each of his conditions. All you have to do is use the right weapon in the right situation.'

"The next moment, the colorful clouds faded and Ghezal was left holding the empty bottle in one hand and a strand of the genii's hair in the other."

The rough voice of a soldier shouting out names for the night shift of torture suddenly interrupted Kojah's tale, and the old man heaved an impatient sigh. His frustration, however, was not nearly as great as those who had to leave this pleasant fantasy for a grim eight hours of torture. As soon as the men had gone, Kojah went back to the story with as much enthusiasm and passionate fervor as before.

"The next morning, the townspeople were awakened by the sound of drums played by the king's slaves, inviting all the people to the castle. It wasn't long before the castle courtyard was full of people who were secretly hoping for the defeat of the cruel king. Outwardly, of course, they had to appear very excited, or they would lose their lives.

"In the middle of this commotion, young Ghezal appeared -- afraid and powerless, but determined that no matter what happened, he would keep the frail torch of his dignity alive, even if he lost his life.

"When King Jaber saw Ghezal, he burst out laughing. 'Is this the person who is challenging me?' he asked in a proud, mocking tone. 'I, Jaber, the king of kings

-- and this is the man who wants to marry my daughter? Just look at him!'

"The huge crowd started to laugh. Poor Ghezal had never been so humiliated in his life, but he spoke not a word. He just stood there, looking at the king whose eyes started burning with flames of rage.

"'Give him the milk!' Jaber ordered.

"Ghezal was handed a tall flagon full of creamy milk. The moment he finished drinking, his entire body began to burn. He felt as if liquid flames were running through his veins, taking over his mind and his feelings. Ghezal didn't know what he was doing. One moment, he was rolling on the ground screaming, and the next, he was running as fast as he could. Suddenly, he found himself on the steep banks of a river. The pain was too much to bear. Horrified, Ghezal watched his body transforming into something hideous. Hair grew all over him. Then he heard himself howling like a wolf. Fire came out of his mouth like a dragon, and he felt the sudden urge to kill and destroy anyone or anything in his way. But something deep down inside quietly told Ghezal that he could control these feelings. Exhausted from the pain and torrent of emotions inside him, the young man made his way toward a deep gorge near the river where he could lie down without being seen.

"Once inside the gorge, Ghezal discovered many bones and the skulls of humans as well as animals. When he lay down, Ghezal saw a serpent arching its coils beside him, and looking straight into his eyes. The serpent bent its head and spit venom into an empty skull. Ghezal felt the temptation to kill growing stronger inside him. All he wanted was to bite off the head of the serpent.

"Ghezal knew he couldn't control himself much longer, and realized if he didn't do something soon, he would become like King Jaber. Picking up the skull full of venom, Ghezal lifted it to his lips and drank every drop.

"The pain grew even sharper than before. Soon he was hallucinating, seeing creatures and monsters more wild and terrible than anyone's imaginings. At last, exhaustion took over all his senses. Ghezal couldn't move or keep his eyes open. All night long he burned with fever and his sleep was tortured with horrible nightmares.

"Dawn was approaching when the nightmares and the fever suddenly left him. Ghezal awoke, amazed that he was still alive. He turned his head to the right, then to the left. There was no pain. He touched his face and squeezed his cheeks. His body felt fine and perfectly whole. Ghezal didn't understand how this could be so after drinking so much poison, but he quickly got up and headed back to the town.

"Everyone was surprised to see the young man, and when the news of Ghezal's triumph reached the ears of the king, he savagely took out his anger on his poor associates. Then he summoned Ghezal and spelled out the terms of the second condition.

"'On the south side of the town is a barn full of wheat. Your task is to remove all the wheat and dump it into a barn on the north end of town. To pass the condition, all this must be accomplished in one night.'

"Ghezal left the castle and made his way to the first barn. Slumping down on the huge pile of wheat, he knew he had been given an impossible task. Then he remembered the creature in the bottle. Ghezal grabbed the strands of hair which he had sewn onto his clothes, and burned it as the creature had instructed. Seconds later, he heard the voice of the invisible genii, who told him to lie down and go to sleep.

"Ghezal was too tired and discouraged to do anything else. When he woke up the next morning, he was surprised to find himself in the barn on the opposite side of town, lying on top of the same pile of wheat where he had fallen asleep the night before. King Jaber was even more surprised to discover that the young man had met and passed his second condition.

"But Ghezal still needed one more miracle in order to complete King Jaber's last condition, which was to bring him the heart of the sorcerers. Ghezal had no knowledge about such things, so once more, he went to see wise old Hakeem.

"'The heart of the sorcerers is a rock,' Hakeem told him. 'If you travel toward the east, after passing seven chains of mountains, you will find a beautiful blue lake. Every night at midnight, something hideous and ugly comes out of the lake with the heart of the sorcerers in its mouth. The rock is so bright that it changes the darkness into daylight. The creature puts the rock on a hilltop, then starts destroying anything and anyone within his reach. How much time did Jaber give you?' Hakeem wanted to know.

"'Only a month,' Ghezal responded.

"'That is plenty of time to do the task,' Hakeem assured him. 'I wish I could go with you, but I'm too old for that. After passing the sixth chain of mountains you will come to the Valley of the Sorcerers. In that valley, you will see and hear a lot of strange things. Remember, if you don't look back, the creatures cannot hurt you. You can eat the fruits of the trees before the Valley of the Sorcerers, but don't eat anything from the valley itself. And make sure you take a mirror and a shovel with you. The creatures are afraid of mirrors. You'll know what to do with the shovel once you get there. When you reach the valley, keep praying, because the creatures cannot harm you while you are thinking about God. At the lake, you'll be safe until midnight, but then you will have to find a place to hide.'

"Ghezal went home and packed everything he thought he could use on the trip. The next morning, he got up very early, and after saying his prayers, started walking toward the east with the shovel in his hand and a pack on his back.

"Except for a few hours of rest and sleep, Ghezal walked day and night. He didn't even think how tired he was. He didn't care how his feet were swelling and hurting, because of his goal. That goal was to end the sorcery in Jaber's kingdom, which had been the cause of such misery in Baharistan.

"After several days, Ghezal arrived on the summit of the sixth mountain. From there, he could see the valley and the lake far below. Both appeared normal and calm, but Ghezal decided to keep a safe distance and spend the night on the mountain.

"As midnight drew closer, the young man grew more anxious. As far as the eye could see, there was nothing but darkness. Then, Ghezal noticed the lake was beginning to shine like crystal. In seconds, the surrounding darkness had brightened into daylight. Suddenly, there was a huge splash and out of the lake emerged a hairy, ugly creature with sharp horns and something bright and shining in its mouth. The creature climbed the hill near the lake, dropped the light on top, then returned to the valley. Once there, he lifted his head and bellowed in a voice as strong as thunder. That sound was like the soul of everything evil. In answer to the beast's bellowing cry, Ghezal heard the howling and screaming of all the other creatures in the valley. It sounded as if they were celebrating the arrival of the devil who was their leader.

"Ghezal watched from his hiding place as the creatures left the valley. He didn't know where they were going or what they were doing. Shortly before dawn, he heard the creatures returning. Ghezal watched as their leader climbed the hill, took the shining rock in his mouth, then returned to the watery depths of the lake just before the sun's rising.

"Ghezal put his pack on his back and walked toward the valley as dawn was breaking. When he entered the valley, he couldn't believe his astonished eyes and ears. Strange faces of people and animals appeared and disappeared before his eyes. He saw skeletons walking about, and trees and flowers growing upside down without any roots in the ground. And there were strange voices. One was the voice of a woman calling, 'You are my son. Look at me. Come and hold me. Let me show you the love of a mother.' Next he heard the voice of his father begging him to look back. At times, the flying, taunting voices were so near he had to close his eyes to avoid them.

"Ghezal kept on playing and walking. He was nearing the end of the valley when he saw a huge chunk of the mountain rolling toward him. Ghezal screamed and closed his eyes. When he opened them, a big pile of dirt and rock had fallen right in front of him. Then he saw a huge wall. The wall changed form until it had eyes, ears, and a huge mouth which kept repeating, 'You're not allowed here! Get out! Get out!'

"Ghezal showed the mirror to the wall, and it disappeared just as suddenly as it had come, but the echoes of laughter and mocking words still surrounded him on all sides.

"Putting his hands on his ears, Ghezal started running as fast as he could. When he neared the lake, everything was still once more. Ghezal splashed some cool water on his face, then climbed to the top of the hill. Without wasting another moment, he began to put his plan of the night before into action. All day long, he dug a deep hole where he could hide after night fell. The day had nearly passed before the job was finished. Ghezal crawled inside, then settled down to wait.

"He was nearly asleep when he saw a bright light appear above his hiding place. Ghezal waited until the creatures had all left the valley, then he climbed out, ran over and grabbed the bright stone, and jumped back inside his hole. When Ghezal put the stone inside his pack, everything immediately went black. When he pulled it out, the dark hole was as bright as day. Ghezal realized that this was the power of the mirror, because mirrors showed the real existence of things. They revealed only the truth.

"Moments later, Ghezal could heard the demon digging the ground with his horns, trying to find the stone. Ghezal huddled inside the hole, clutching his pack, hardly daring to breathe.

"Once the sun came up, everything was quiet. Ghezal climbed out of the hole and witnessed a thick, terrible smoke rising from the remains of the demon who had burned under the magnificent rays of the sun.

"During the long journey home, Ghezal was no longer frightened, because he knew he held the power and the heart of magic in his hand. As soon as he returned, King Jaber was knocking on Ghezal's door, begging him for the stone.

"'Here is the Princess,' the king said. 'You've passed all the conditions and now you can marry her. You can even take my kingdom. Just give me the stone.'

"'I didn't do this for your daughter,' Ghezal told King Jaber. 'Nor for your kingdom. I did it to save the people of Beharistan.'

"The news of Bhezal's triumph soon spread throughout the kingdom. Every one, including old Hakeem, wanted to see the hero of Beharistan.

"'I have waited a long time to see the man who had all the qualities to defeat the demon,' Hakeem told Ghezal.

'I knew that you were the one the first time you came to me. I have watched you and followed you everywhere. The battle that you have won, wasn't only between you and the king. It was a battle between good and evil. Jaber was testing your strength the first time he saw you. By laughing and making fun of your appearance, Jaber was trying to give you a reason to be angry and react foolishly. Instead, you were patient. That made him so furious you could see the rage in his eyes. Jaber realized his defeat at that moment and wanted to make you one of them. The milk he gave you was mixed with his blood. When you went to the gorge, Jaber and his demons were all there to celebrate their victory and watch your destruction, but you were in too much pain to notice them.

"'Then Jaber transformed himself into a serpant and offered you the cure for his poison. He thought you would never take the cure, because life is too sweet. You took it for unselfish reasons because you didn't want to harm any one. Your sense of sacrifice saved your life. After that, Jaber was so desperate, he thought of something humanly impossible by asking you to transport the wheat. You needed a miracle to accomplish this. Your respect and compassion for all things provided you with the way to get the help of Jaber's enemy to make this possible.

"'Finally, the king created a situation in which he thought he would win either way. If you brought him the stone, Jaber would have the power that he wanted, and if you got destroyed on the way, it would still be his triumph. But with your courage and wisdom, the power of your beliefs and the control of your senses, you brought the demon to his knees.' Hakeem smiled into Ghezal's face and told him, 'The weapons you used were patience, belief in God, compassion, courage, a sense of sacrifice and self-control. That is all you needed to beat Jaber. Now the only thing left to do is to destroy the stone and replace the king.'

"After saying this, Hakeem ground the stone from a big mirror into powder, and while the entire town watched, he threw the powder into the river. Minutes later, the townspeople witnessed a huge cyclone coming from the east which disappeared in the heart of the river. Cheering the end of sorcery, everyone in town was chanting the name of Hakeem as their new leader.

"Ghezal, who loved nature, wanted to continue the profession of his father. One day he was working in the forest when he saw someone coming toward him. It was the Princess Henah, who said to him, 'The man who saved Behiristan is the right man for me to marry."

"Ghezal hesitated a little, then thought to himself. I have experienced fear, pain and loneliness, but I have never experienced the love of a woman and the pleasure of having children.

"All the inhabitants of Beharistan were invited to the castle for the wedding celebration of Princess Henah and Ghezal. As the people were leaving the castle after the wedding, they noticed a beautiful white flag with green writing flying from the highest ramparts of the castle. It read: Happiness and Goodness go hand in hand. No matter where you throw goodness, it will always shine."

Kojah nodded at us and smiled. "God granted the wishes of these people. May he grant ours."

Chapter 15

*"If you don't see an ocean of pain and
emotions on the eyelash,
Then you don't know the depth of a single
tear."*

Indian Saying

ONE MORNING, ABOUT two weeks after Kojah's arrival, I was busy painting Communist slogans in one of the Investigator's offices when I heard the cries of a baby. I stood very still, listening with shock and disbelief. The sound seemed to be coming from the next room. Moments later, the baby's cries were joined by the screams of a woman. Without thinking, I grabbed my bucket of paint and quickly left the room. Once outside, I tried to make it appear that I was mixing the paint, then crept over to the window of the next room. My shocked mind had a brief glimpse of a little baby lying on the floor and nearby, the naked feet of a woman wrapped with electrical wires.

The sight was so horrifying, I didn't know what to do. Grabbing the bucket of paint, I hurried back to the office where I had been working, and started slopping the paint on the wall.

I tried to block the images from my mind, but I couldn't block the sounds. The more I heard the baby's cries and the mother's screams, the more upset I became. Soon, red paint was dripping down the wall from my shaking brush, and my legs were so weak I could hardly stand.

I sank down on the floor with my back against the wall and my hands on my knees. Putting my face in my hands, I rubbed my eyes with clenched fists. Then the tears came, pouring down my cheeks, and I heard myself sobbing.

"Oh, God! These little children ... this woman ... no one is safe from these people. What is this?"

I don't know how long I sat there crying and talking angrily to God for allowing such horrible things to happen to our people. When I heard a sudden noise behind the locked door, I jumped to my feet and reached for the paint brush.

Whoever was at the door must have had another key, because seconds later, the door opened and one of the Investigators entered the room.

"If you're finished in here, we need you to paint another office," he said. "They're still working in there, so don't get in the way."

Still shaken, I picked up the can of paint and blindly followed him to the designated room. A soldier answered my knock, telling me to come in and get to work. As I entered, I saw an old man with a long silver beard and a white turban around his head. He was lying on the floor and the wires from the electrical machine were hooked to his shaking toes.

I bit down hard on my bottom lip and started to paint, while the Investigator and the soldiers continued their cruel business. As I worked, I had to listen to their rough voices asking the old man over and over again, "Did you do it?" "What are their names?" "Who asked you to give them the weapons?"

From the Investigators' questions, I assumed the man must have been involved in arms trading, but no matter what they did to him, his answer was always the same. "*Allah toba ... Allah toba ....* " which means, "God forgive me."

His courage and will power amazed me. I was painting in that room for nearly three hours and throughout the entire time, the man's answer never varied. Never before had I witnessed such strength, especially in someone so old.

The more the Investigators tortured him, the more I found myself wanting to stop them. But what could I do? Against the soldiers with their machine guns, I was totally helpless.

As the hours dragged on, the soldiers' frustration and anger grew. They were swearing and throwing things around the room, but the old man was oblivious to all this. He was totally out of the physical world. What I had tried to do weeks earlier when I was under the torture, by refusing to live in the present time, he was doing on a much deeper level with the name of Allah. The old man was in another dimension where there wasn't any pain and where his soul was connected to the highest power above the skies. His eyes were staring at the ceiling, as if he were having some kind of supernatural vision.

Finally, the Investigators began kicking him and the old man passed out. Two soldiers grabbed his hands and dragged his unconscious body from the room.

When my work was finished, I returned to my room, but I couldn't get the day's horrible sights and sounds out of my mind. The cries of that baby and the screams of the mother ... her naked feet wrapped with bare wires ... the eyes of the old man and his trembling voice repeating ... "*Allah tobah ... Allah tobah ....* "

Usually, my evenings were spent talking with other prisoners, listening to stories and being with my friends. But this night, I didn't want to talk to anyone. All around me, I could hear the voices of the men who were under torture, but I wasn't with them any more. I just lay there thinking and thinking .... What was it that gave that old man the power to be in so much pain and still not utter a word of complaint? The only answer I could find was the name of *Allah* and the belief the old man had in Him.

The next day, I wanted to talk with someone about this, but most of my roommates were new prisoners. Arjung had been moved to another room, Quassim was gone, and Kojah was in too much pain from his recent torture sessions to talk. The only other familiar face was Noor, whom I knew from school. I crawled over beside him and after sharing my thoughts, Noor answered that anyone could have this kind of power, if he really gives himself to God and believes in Him totally.

"Why don't you start praying," he suggested.

I thought about this, and knew he was right. "From now on," I told him, "I'm not going to miss any prayers. I'm going to pray five times a day like any good Moslem, no matter what happens."

As Noor and I were talking, the soldiers brought a wounded boy of perhaps fourteen or fifteen into the room. His clothes were covered with blood and he was so thin he looked more like a skeleton than a human being. There was scarcely any meat or muscle on his bones, and his face was so white I wondered if he had any blood left in his body.

Someone asked him what had happened, and all he could say was, "A bomb .... " After examining the boy, we discovered two bullets and some metal shrapnel were still in his body. No attempt had been made to treat his wounds.

We didn't really know how to help him. We only knew we had to do something. A few prisoners tore off pieces of their clothes for bandages and we tried as best we could to wrap his wounds and stop the bleeding. The boy's clothes were filthy and reeked of rotten blood. After giving him something to wrap around himself, I carried the bloody clothes outside for washing. There wasn't any soap, only the hose. After digging a hole in the dirt, I filled it with water and put his clothes in to soak. After a few minutes of soaking, I started rinsing and rubbing them against a rock. God knows how much I squeezed, rubbed and beat those clothes. After working for nearly three hours, I still couldn't get all the stains out, but at least they looked and smelled better.

All that night the boy was burning up with fever and talking nonsense. Sometimes, he was screaming and crying. Every time I heard his cries, I felt the heat of anger rising inside me, because we were so helpless to ease his pain.

Early the next morning, around five a.m., I got up and joined the inmates who were praying in a corner of the yard. The stars were still visible in that beautiful square sky, and as I prayed, the anger left me. I didn't care what happened to me any more. Inside, I just felt peaceful. Prayer took all the fears away.

When Awaz arrived two hours' later to call us for work, he was furious that the young boy lying so still didn't obey his commands. The guard stood over him, shouting insults and insisting that he get up and go to work. The boy was too weak from loss of blood to move, much less go to work.

Awaz raised his baton to strike him, and suddenly, I couldn't remain silent any longer. "He can't get up!" I cried. "Look at him! He's dying!"

The guard gave me a dirty look and stalked out of the room, to return a few minutes later, accompanied by the warden and another soldier.

No one said a word as they examined the boy, then carried him out, but the sadness in the room was a tangible weight felt by us all.

* * *

A few nights later, Kojah was telling us a story around midnight, when we heard soldiers bringing someone into the small room next to ours. Ordinarily, this room was empty, but when someone was in really bad shape they would put him in there. After the soldiers had left, I heard the man moaning. It was hard to understand his words, but I thought it was something like *Allah* or *Aow,* which means water.

Hearing his moans, I knew I had to do something. For days, I had been feeling guilty and ashamed whenever I thought about that old man, the woman and that baby. I don't know what I could have done to help them, but I should have done something. Perhaps it was these feelings of guilt and shame, or maybe I was just tired of being so helpless, but something gave me the courage to act.

Prisoners weren't allowed to stand up in the room at night, so I told Kojah to watch from the corner of the window and warn me if he saw someone coming by coughing as loud as he could. Then, with a glass of water in one hand, I started crawling on my elbows toward the small room.

Inside, I found a young man lying on the floor. He was covered with blood and his face had so many cuts, all I could make out of his features were his big brown eyes. God knows what else they did to him.

I put his head on my arm, then soaked one of the corners of my shirt in the glass of water and started wiping off the blood. Then I saw his face. Oh, my God ... what a handsome man.

He couldn't talk, but his lips and his eyes were moving very slowly. I tried to clean his mouth so I could give him some water, but he couldn't swallow. The water mixed with the blood, and ran out of his mouth.

I was trying to make him more comfortable when I saw one of his fingers move. I thought he wanted something. Putting a hand under his head, I looked down into his face. With effort, the man's eyes rolled slowly upward to meet mine.

A single drop of tear came from the corner of one eye, slipped down the cuts on his face and hovered on his earlobe before dropping on my hand. By the time it reached my hand, that tear was as red as his blood.

Then, suddenly, he just stopped breathing. I couldn't believe this was happening. It was the first time someone had died in my arms.

With my arm around the man's shoulder, I leaned over and kissed his forehead. It was very cold. I put his head down and took his hand to feel his pulse, but there wasn't any. I closed his eyes and his mouth, while tears ran down my cheeks and fell on his young face, which I cleaned for the last time.

I got to my feet without fear of being seen or shot and returned to the room. No one asked any questions because the answer was already written on my face.

A few hours later, I heard soldiers in the hall. Silently, I watched as they wrapped the young man's body in a blanket and carried him out of the prison.

Sleep did not come that night. For some reason, that last look and that last tear ... changed me. There hadn't been a word between us, only a glance and a single tear, yet somehow, I could feel his deepest emotions. I understood his pain and his sorrow. I knew how much he wanted to have a human being next to him in the last moments of his life. I had no idea whether he saw me as a member of his family, a friend or as an angel, but during that time, I felt like his closest friend and brother.

Without knowing the man's name or anything about him, I was left with a sad, but profound memory to remind me that all human beings, no matter how different we seem to be, are all alike once we remove the thick curtain that blinds our truer, deeper vision of one another. For a brief moment that curtain was removed from my eyes, and I knew that long before we became Christians, Moslems or Communists, we were brothers and sisters by the power of the most sacred word: humanity. During that moment, I determined that no doctrine, religion or power had the right to treat another life the way his was treated.

In the nights to come, our little square sky was invaded by those two silent, yet whispering eyes, challenging me to tell the story of a single tear. A tear that became the language of a last beating heart. And I knew if I ever got out of this place, I would share the effect of the unforgettable stain of that tear in my hand with the world.

Chapter 16

FOR DAYS AFTER that young man died in my arms, I was deep in my thoughts. Only prayer and the strength that comes from God gave me any comfort. Kneeling in the yard with hundreds of other men, feeling their faith and unity, I felt peaceful inside. Prayer took away the pain and eased the horror of that place, but it couldn't take away the sadness when names were called and friends left us.

One night around midnight, a soldier came with a long list of names, and Kojah's was among those that were called. The old man and I had grown very close during the time he was with us. He had even promised me a job in his company if we were ever released. But this was not to be.

We bid our storyteller goodbye with embraces, tears, and the heartfelt words, "May God bless you."

After Kojah had gone, the room felt colder and strangely empty, in spite of those who remained. For the few weeks he was with us, the old man lit the candle of hope in our hearts and our minds. And like the lullaby of a mother to her children, Kojah's fairy tales made us go to our deepest sleep and dream about the good things that existed outside of our life behind bars.

The next day, I was mixing paint in the yard when I saw a familiar face. It was Riza, the KhAD agent who had arrested me so many months before.

"How are you doing?" Riza stopped to ask, as if we were old acquaintances meeting on the street.

"Do you remember telling me that you were going to let me go after some questioning?" I said. "Well, I'm still here."

"You didn't really believe that, did you?" Riza responded with a twisted smile.

I looked at him and shook my head. "I guess not. Were you the one who arrested my brother Hafiz?"

"I'm not supposed to tell you anything," Riza replied, "but I know they won't let you go because you know too many of us."

Riza walked past me, then paused. "Your brother is alive," he said quietly, and continued on his way.

Something in his voice and eyes made me feel he was telling the truth. I went back to mixing the paint, feeling a welcome lightness inside just knowing my brother was still alive.

Minutes later, Arjung approached me with a big smile on his face.

"What is going on, Arjung?"

"You won't believe this!" the older man answered trying to contain his excitement. "Don't tell anyone, but I recently made an interesting tableau for one of the prison officials. I used a little bit of my talent and imagination and drew a picture of their leader in one corner with a sunset and lots of revolutionary red clouds, along with some slogans and poems I knew they would like. I gave it to him last night. He was so impressed, he told me I could have anything I wanted -- except for my freedom. 'Then you can't give me what I want,' I answered, and he said, 'Try me.'"

Arjung's eager face and shining eyes made me smile. "So what did you ask for?"

"I told him I wanted to see my family for one hour. At first he said that was impossible, so I told him to forget it. Then this morning he came to my room to tell me he'd made the arrangements to take me to my house tonight." Arjung put a hand on my shoulder and sighed. "Today is going to be a very long day for me."

The next morning when I saw Arjung, he looked pale and sad, but he was shaved and wearing nice clean clothes.

Before I could ask him anything he said, "What a mistake. I just poured tons of salt on my wounds."

"Is everything okay at home?"

"Yes, everybody's fine. They were thrilled to see me, but when I had to leave, everyone was crying."

I looked at the tears slipping down his face and told him softly, "I don't know what's going to happen to us, but at least you had the chance to say your last goodbyes to them." I gave Arjung's neat appearance a startled second glance. "Arjung, you've shaved and changed your clothes! Don't you think that will make the guards suspicious?"

He clapped a hand to his mouth, looking suddenly amazed. "Oh, God, I never even thought of that! When I went home, after a few minutes, my family couldn't stand my dirty clothes and stinky body, so they asked me to take a shower." Arjung's bushy brows narrowed in a frown. "What should we do?"

"Let's rub some mud on your clothes and put a little black paint on your face," I suggested.

Arjung gave me a sheepish grin and we soon had him looking respectably dirty like all the other prisoners.

A week after that incident, Arjung was gone. The soldiers didn't call his name at the dangerous time of night, and I hadn't heard it in the morning. It was as if he simply disappeared.

A few days following Arjung's disappearance, Noor's name was called in the afternoon, along with several others. I felt grateful, knowing he was being transferred to Pol-i-Charkhi, but I missed my friends.

In the beginning, hearing the prisoners' names called out by the soldiers had filled me with terror. Life was so precious. But having that young man die in my arms changed how I felt. If he could do it, so could I. Sometimes, I even found myself silently praying that my name would be on one of those lists. One by one they had been taken away or killed. Ibrahim. Daghar-Wal. Sediq. Kojah. And Quassim. Now my friends Arjung and Noor were gone as well. The only familiar face left in the room was Jan Mohammed, the mechanic.

With Arjung gone, there was no further painting to be done, so I was sent back to work in the yard for the

Mason. I had no idea what month or day it was, but the shortness of the days and the bitter cold told me that winter must be coming on. Several times in recent weeks, snow had fallen from that beautiful square sky. On especially cold days, I wondered if my sport coat was enough to keep Sediq warm. That is, if he were still alive. I still had Ibrahim's blue sweater, but I hesitated wearing it, knowing he had intended it for his wife.

Early one morning, before Awaz arrived to summon us for work, a soldier came to the door and called my name. He didn't have a list of any names other than mine. My heart began pounding with the old familiar fear, as I got up and followed the soldier down the hall. After all this time, I couldn't understand why my name was being called. Was it more torture? Or death.

The answer seemed painfully clear when the guard delivered me to one of the torture rooms and knocked on the door.

The room was approximately 15 x 25 feet in size and poorly furnished, with a few chairs against one wall, and a desk situated close to the window, to give the Investigator a clear view of the yard.

I stood in the doorway, squinting at the dark outline of a man sitting behind the desk. Memories of those horrible weeks when I had been under torture came flooding back. Whenever I was taken to a torture room in the morning, it usually took a moment to see the Investigator's face because of the sunlight streaming through the window behind him. This initial glimpse of a dark profile behind the desk was often more frightening than the demonic faces which haunted my dreams at night.

As my eyes grew accustomed to the light, I recognized the familiar features of someone with whom I had shared the classrooms and hallways of the University of Kabul.

His name was Sabur. A tall, thin Afghan with green eyes and light brown hair, the man had a reputation among prisoners and Investigators alike for being especially cruel and inventive when it came to devising new methods of torture. His diabolical acts had even earned him the dubious distinction of a special title: *Son of Cruel.*

Less than one year ago, he and I had attended college together. I was in the French department and Sabur was studying Pashtu. We saw each other frequently in the halls, and although we weren't close friends, we often ate lunch in the same cafeteria.

Now Sabur was one of them.

It was common practice to have three soldiers in the torture room to assist the Investigator in torturing the prisoner. I had my next shock when we entered the room. Sabur told the soldiers to leave, then shut and locked the door.

"Sit down," he said, gesturing to the cement floor which was carpeted with a fine Afghan rug. Most of the other torture rooms were covered by a cheap, thin material called *gilam.* Only a few had the luxury of an Afghan rug, depending upon the importance of the occupant. Whether the floors were covered with fine carpets or shabby *gilam,* they all had some things in common. In addition to the dirt, they were stained with matted, dried blood.

I sat down cross-legged on the rug, and Sabur instructed me to put the wires from the electrical machine on my toes.

Nervously, I did as he asked.

"Would you like some tea?" Sabur asked, offering me a cup.

I took the tea, feeling suspicious and totally bewildered by his actions. I hadn't noticed until now that the messy assortment of papers and files on his desk had been pushed to one side to allow space for a teapot, two cups, and a small plate of *nuqul* (frosted almonds).

"Do you want some candy?" he asked a moment later.

I didn't really want any, but because he offered it, I took one of the candied almonds and put it in my mouth.

What the hell is going on? I wondered. Are they trying to change their way? Maybe this is some new method to get to me.

The next moment, Sabur turned on a cassette recorder and suddenly, I got goose bumps all over my body. The song on the tape was one of my favorites, sung by the Indian singer LaTa.

The first time I'd heard this particular song, I was passing by a restaurant on my way home from college. Instantly, it captured my attention and I stopped to listen. I loved the song so much that I went inside the restaurant and asked the owner if he would be willing to sell it to me.

"No, I love that song, too, and I don't want to sell it," he had answered.

"Would you be willing to make a copy of it for me?" I wanted to know. "I'll be happy to pay you."

"No, just forget it," he said and waved me away.

I left his restaurant feeling very disappointed, but by the time I got home, I already had a plan. I loved Indian music and had dozens of cassette tapes in my collection. That night I recorded a tape of some songs that were very similar in style to the one I wanted. The next day, I went back to the restaurant owner. "I know you don't want to sell that song that I liked so much, but would you please listen to this?"

"Sure," he said and took the tape. After a few minutes, he told me he loved the tape and wanted to know where he could get one.

I smiled at the owner. "Just record that one song for me and I'll be happy to give you this tape."

Now, here I was in a torture prison, and an Investigator who used to be a college friend was playing that very same song.

"Life can be a desert, or life can be a garden.
If you swim in the ocean of love,
life can be the most beautiful flower you've ever seen.
The person that fights and plays with the storm is the one who will reach the shore, because difficulties are afraid of a strong person.

> *If you have the right path and the right support,*
> *life can be the best hope---- "*

Sabur noticed the sudden change in my expression and asked, "What's wrong?"

"Nothing," I said. "It's just that I love this song very much ...."

When the song ended, Sabur turned off the tape and leaned forward to face me. "I know what you're thinking," he said, "but you don't have to worry. I'm not going to torture you. All this is just for show. In fact, I'm going to tell you something. I know we knew each other. Last night they gave me your case, and told me to do it either way. Just finish it." Sabur paused, then told me, "When I went home, it was bothering me because I knew you, and I knew you hadn't done anything wrong. I even talked about it with my wife. I told her they'd given me your case and that I had to torture you." He sighed and shook his head. "We talked about it for a long time, and I finally decided that I can't do it."

Knowing Sabur's reputation, I'm sure my expression was skeptical, as well as shocked.

"I have a two-year-old son," he went on. "Last night, when my wife and I were talking, she told me: 'We both know that you might not be here much longer. After you're gone, what am I going to tell your son so he will remember you? That his father was a murderer of innocent people ... that he tortured other mother's sons and sent them to their death ....'" Sabur looked at me, his green eyes full of anger as well as pain. "And it's not only that. The reason we did this -- the reason we became Communists -- we wanted to build the country. We wanted to help people ... the same people we're torturing now." He slammed a frustrated fist on the desk. "They tricked us! They played with our feelings. Now, it's too late. I can't go back to my old life, and I can't join the rebels. I hate being one of them and doing these things ...."

Part of me was still wondering if there might be some other motive behind what he was saying. Sabur seemed sincere, but it was difficult to believe that an Investigator was telling me these things.

"I don't know what to tell you," I said finally. I'm really shocked ... and surprised ...."

Sabur's mouth twisted in a bitter smile. "I know you don't trust me."

I nodded. "Yes, that's true. I don't trust you."

The lines of his mouth tightened with sudden determination. "They gave me your case to finish it one way or the other," he said. "But I'm going to help you. Whenever you hear noises in the hall, I want you to scream as loud as you can."

For the next eight hours, Sabur and I sat in his office and talked. We talked about his family, about his dreams for the country and the problems in the Communist party. He ordered food for himself, and shared it with me. Whenever we heard a sound in the hall, I would start screaming and he grabbed the machine, to make it look like I was being tortured.

At the end of the shift, he said, "It's time for you to go, but in order to write my report, we're going to have to do the same thing tomorrow."

All those times that I had been inside the torture rooms with their white walls and blood red slogans, fear was the conqueror of my heartbeat, and when I left, anger and shame were always stronger than my pain.

This time, I left his room in a daze of confusion, not knowing what to think.

The next morning, two soldiers brought me back to Sabur's office. Just as he had the day before, Sabur told the soldiers they could go, then locked the door and invited me to sit down.

"I brought you another tape," he said pleasantly, putting it in the cassette player.

After listening to the music for a while, he turned it off, then told me, "Okay, today we're going to do something. Come here. I want you to read what I'm going to write."

I stood next to the desk, as Sabur took a pen and started to write. There were certain codes and abbreviations that I didn't understand, but in effect, he was stating that he had done certain kinds of torture to me and had been unable to find out anything. My heartbeat quickened and I felt cold sweat bead on my forehead when he turned to the last page of my file.

Staring down at that final page, I remembered all those I had read with the decision "condemned to death," written in red ink. I felt as if I must be dreaming as he wrote that I was innocent and should be set free. Then he signed his name.

"There's nothing else they can do," Sabur assured me. "This was their last chance. They gave me your case because they know I've made a lot of people cry and confess, but I can't do it to you." He looked at me and said quietly, "I may not be here tomorrow or the next day ... I don't know ... but I'm not going to live my life like this."

I left Sabur's office with a sense of awe and gratitude, knowing that the man who should have been my executioner, had turned out to be my savior instead.

* * *

Days passed and I heard nothing more from Sabur or any of the prison officials. Life continued as before.

One winter afternoon, I was working in the yard when a soldier called a few of us to come and empty a truck full of bricks. While I was working, I glanced across the way and noticed a man sitting alone in a small room. It was Sabur. His hands and feet were chained, and he had positioned himself in a corner nearest the window to feel a little sun. Sabur must have been watching me for some time, but I hadn't been aware of him until now. The moment I looked his way, Sabur gave me a big smile and said, "You're still here?"

I approached the window of his room. "Oh my God, what happened to you?"

"I told you ... I couldn't do this any more. I made the mistake of sharing these feelings with some friends and one of them reported me. That's why I'm here."

I didn't know what to say to him. In spite of what he had done to others, it made me feel bad seeing him like that.

A few days later, the soldiers came to our room at a very unusual time -- early in the afternoon -- and read a list of thirty-four names. Mine was the twenty-fourth name on the list. The soldiers instructed those of us whose names had been called to get our belongings and come with them.

I was nervous, but not afraid as we followed the soldiers across the yard, down a long hall and into a large room near the prison's main entrance. Here, we were given forms to fill out and told that after dinner, the President of KhAD was going to speak to us. Then we would be set free.

Everyone was so happy and excited at this news, there was no way we could eat dinner. And if we'd had any choice in the matter, we certainly didn't want to wait around to listen to a boring speech given by Asidullah Amin. We just wanted to leave! Since we had no choice, the thirty-four of us sat on the floor, excitedly talking about our future and what we wanted to do. Some of the men talked about how wonderful it would be to see their children or grandchildren again. Others were eager to get a job. And a few were so disillusioned by the situation in Afghanistan, that they planned to leave the country. Thinking about my own plans once I was reunited with my family, I told the others that one of the things I wanted most was to get my graduation certificate from the University of Kabul, which had been denied me because of my arrest.

Everyone was smiling and joking. Our excitement seemed to fill that dreary room with warmth and light.

The dinner hour passed and we were still waiting for the President of KHAD to arrive. As more minutes dragged by, the dark clouds of impatience and fear began invading the daylight of our hopes. No one understood what had happened or why we weren't being released, but when the nine o'clock curfew passed and we still hadn't received any word, we all knew it wasn't going to happen. Disappointment hung heavy in the room's silence as our shared hopes for the future now became our shared misery.

The long night passed and few if any had more than an hour or two's restless sleep. When breakfast was brought by the guards, no one had any appetite. The night before we had been too excited to eat. Now, we were too disappointed.

The day crawled slowly into afternoon. Outside the window, I could see flakes of snow falling from a gray sky, and still we waited.

It was late afternoon when the guard Ahmad Shah entered our room and motioned for me to come talk to him.

"What's going on?" I asked. "I thought we were supposed to be released."

"You have the world's worst luck," he told me. "Before you can be released, the President of KhAD has to sign your papers, and he'll never sign them now. Last night, Asidullah Amin was shot!"

Chapter 17

WHEN I SHARED Ahmad Shah's news with the other men, their feelings were as frustrated as mine, but we were also very relieved. At least now we had a reason for what had happened. Our future was still uncertain, but even this small crumb of knowledge was better than nothing at all.

A short time later, an armed guard entered the room, and without any words of explanation, ordered us to make a line and follow him. Of all the dread and uncertainty I had experienced during the past twenty-four hours, that moment was the worst. Everyone knew that before inmates could be released, they were given forms called "promise slips" to sign, and as yet, we had signed nothing.

Silently, we filed out of the room, not knowing where we were going or what our fate might be. The soldier led us down the prison halls and outside where a large truck with canvas sides was waiting. Other guards with machine guns stood nearby. Our final destination was still a mystery, but when the guards shouted for us to get inside the truck, one thing was clear. We were leaving *Sedarat*.

After all thirty-four inmates had climbed in the back, the canvas was closed and secured. The blackness surrounding us was as dark as a tomb. Moments later, the engine started and we were on our way to God knows where. As the truck rumbled along, everyone was fumbling about in the darkness, trying to find a hole in the canvas or a screw to loosen. Jan Mohammed was the first to succeed and in less than five minutes, there were at least half a dozen other holes through which we took turns looking at the outside world.

The truck had just stopped at a busy intersection when my turn came. The first thing to meet my gaze was a woman's legs from her black high heels up to the knees as she walked along the sidewalk. Sex was the furthest thing from my mind, but the sight of those beautiful, soul-touching legs set my thoughts racing. My emotions and imagination were soaring so high, I felt like I was hallucinating.

Women! What beautiful creatures. They possess the most gracious and feminine names and they have the most sacred knot and bond with men. A mother. A daughter. A sister. A wife and a lover. To honor their existence, millions of poems have been written in every language and in every culture. When men are blessed with their pure love, our feelings and emotions become like the highest, wildest waterfall that joins the calmness of the ocean.

Women ... I salute your miraculous birth into our life from the beginning of time until the end. You nourished us with the essence of life when we were hungry; you taught us how to speak when we were mute, and how to walk when we were crippled. When we were weak and sad and needed sympathy, you shared with us the precious pearls of your kind and beautiful eyes. No matter how strong or weak, how rich or poor, or how young or old a man might be; no matter what race or religion he has -- in a woman's powerful, yet delicate and soft arms, men are like newborns seeking love, nourishment and strength.

Women ... you are the goddesses of love, the queens of giving and forgiveness. In your deep eyes a man can find his soul, and through your hearts he can feel the existence of God.

The beautiful vision was wrested away as the truck moved forward with a gutteral grinding of gears, and another inmate eagerly took my place.

After being on the road for some time, it was obvious that we were not going to be released. The general consensus among the men was that we were heading for Pol-e-Charkhi, the big prison some twelve kilometers outside Kabul.

When our dark journey ended, I climbed out of the truck with the other inmates, and discovered we were inside a large prison compound surrounded by high walls and watchtowers. Directly in front of us was a massive gate with iron bars. Through the bars, I could see a large courtyard and several prisoners running toward us with curious eyes.

I had heard many stories about Pol-e-Charkhi. The monstrous prison had been built in the time of President Daoud, and as the old saying goes, "the tomb digger is the first one in the tomb." Ironically, some of Daoud's relatives and associates were among the first innocents to begin the horrific legends in those dark tombs called the cells of Pol-e-Charkhi.

Looking up at the huge, multi-storied building, I couldn't help but wonder what sort of chapters my own stay would write upon the walls of this place.

The winter sun shone weakly overhead, as we lined up outside the gate. One by one, inmates' names were called, and they were given entry to the prison through a small door next to the gate.

I was looking through the iron bars at the men milling about inside, when I saw my brother Hafiz standing not ten feet away. He was holding the bars with both hands, his eyes anxiously studying the faces of the newcomers.

During my months at *Sedarat*, I had grown a long beard and my hair hung down past my shoulders. In addition, I had lost so much weight that it was little wonder Hafiz wasn't able to recognize me. One glance at his face told me of the frustration and disappointment he must be feeling after waiting and hoping for so long to see his brother come out of that "legendary" truck from *Sedarat*.

Here I was, only a few feet away, and he couldn't hear my heart's excited beating or smell the fragrance of my unlimited happiness at seeing him again. Finally, with a trembling voice, I called out his name.

Hafiz's eyes widened in shock and surprise, and his hands clutched the bars so tightly they were white and bloodless. Moving closer, I could even see the gooseflesh on his arms. I was shaking myself with the excitement and happiness shared between two fortunate brothers. Two brothers, who by the power of God, were offered another chance to celebrate the simplest truths of their birthright -- their brotherhood.

At last, the soldiers called my name. I don't think there could have been another man who entered Pol-e-Charkhi prison as eagerly as I did that day. Hafiz was waiting close by as I came through the door next to the gate.

We fell into each other's arms, hugging each other and crying. Then he grabbed my hands and said in an emotion-choked voice, "Oh, my God! You're alive! You don't know what that means to me!"

He was squeezing my hands so hard, I finally had to tell him, "Would you please let the blood flow through. You're strangling my poor fingers."

Hafiz laughed through his tears and hugged me again.

The next moment, men I had never seen before in my life were coming up to me, shaking my hands and hugging me. They told me how much they had heard about me from my brother, and how worried he had been about my life. I was overwhelmed with happiness.

In the crowd of prisoners, I also discovered some familiar faces of men I had known at *Sedarat*. Noor was there. And Sediq, whose eyes were practically healed. He hadn't regained his full eye sight, but they looked much better. Another welcome face was that of Dr. Habib, the man whose file I had read months before.

My eyes continued to search the prison yard for the three people I was hoping most to see -- Ibrahim, Kojah and Arjung -- but there was no sign of them. When I asked Hafiz if he had heard of these men, he told me no. Then, seeing the sadness on my face, he quickly changed the subject.

"We have three recesses a day and each one lasts about an hour," he said. "During that time, prisoners are allowed to move around the yard and visit with each other."

As the two of us walked around the prison yard, I couldn't help laughing when I saw some of the inmates sitting down, examining their clothes for lice and bugs. Especially the ones with shaved heads. They reminded me of monkeys, searching the heads and bodies of their young ones.

Moments later, I heard a shrill ringing. Hafiz explained this was the warning bell that our recess period was over.

As inmates began returning to their cells, I counted at least twenty soldiers with machine guns, making sure everyone went back inside. Political prisoners were kept on a different level of the prison than regular criminals, Hafiz told me. But as far as assigning inmates to a specific cell, the prison was so overcrowded that the guards didn't care who ended up where, as long as everyone was locked up at the end of the recess.

The prison complex was like a great wheel composed of multi-storied blocks. On the way to Hafiz' cell, we passed through four little iron doors, one on each level and hall. The halls themselves were very long, with small cells on either side. The floor and walls of the individual cells were rough cement with no covering or furniture of any kind.

Prisoners had decorated many of the walls by writing poems, and verses of the Holy Koran. On some walls, I glimpsed the last words of inmates who had already faced their destiny, leaving behind a small trace of their presence in the history book of Pol-e-Charkhi.

Five men already occupied the cramped 4' x 5' space in Hafiz's cell, so there really wasn't room for me. Before I could mention anything, one of the men kindly said, "I'm sure you two brothers have a lot to talk about. I'll leave and stay with one of my friends."

Not long after he had gone, the soldiers checked each cell and put heavy locks on the steel doors.

After they left, Hafiz sat down, and took a pair of very old scissors from his pocket. Political prisoners were not allowed to possess such items, so Hafiz had surreptiously borrowed the scissors from one of the criminals on a lower level.

"Criminals are given lots of privileges that we don't have," one of the other cellmates told me, "Besides that, they seem to have a way of getting what they want, whether it's a pair of scissors, a newspaper, or even a radio."

Hafiz asked me to sit down beside him, then proceeded to give me the worst haircut of my life.

After he had finished, my brother smiled and handed me a broken pocket mirror so I could look at his best work of art.

My mouth fell open at the sight of my newly chopped hair. "It looks like I have prehistoric writing all over my head," I told him.

"Don't worry, it will grow," Hafiz replied.

I ran a hand over my head then handed him the broken mirror. "Now I know why some of the inmates have their heads shaved."

Hafiz laughed but I could see a few tears shining in his eyes. "At least you look like a human being again."

During my days at Pol-e-Charkhi, I often heard prisoners complaining about conditions there. There was ample cause for these complaints, but after the horrible months at *Sedarat*, this place seemed like a five-star hotel. Each new prisoner was given a blanket, a toothbrush and toothpaste, and a bucket to wash his clothes in. One of my greatest pleasures was seeing a bar of soap after nearly six months. I touched it. Then smelled it. Real soap! To me, it had the perfume of the garden of Eden. We even had the luxury of toilet paper, some playing cards and a chess board.

At first glance, the chess pieces seemed very unusual. Then I discovered the inmates had made them themselves, out of toothpaste mixed with paint and the soft insides of bread. In order to get the variety of shapes necessary for the game, the doughy mixture was pushed through different-shaped holes in plastic bottles, something like a primitive cake decorating kit. Afterwards, the chess pieces were put outside in the sun for two or three days to dry. The finished product looked very nice and colorful.

The food at Pol-e-Charkhi was not nice or colorful. For lunch, we were served a watery broth with a hint of vegetables, and for dinner, bland white rice. The most exciting items on our menu were raw onions and fresh jalepenos that we bought from the prison cantina. We didn't have any knives or forks, so we had to smash the onions with our fists, then divide them among us. No matter how hard we brushed our teeth afterwards, we never could get rid of our onion breath. But since this was the only tasty gourmet item on our so-called dinner table (which consisted of some newspaper spread on the cement floor), we wouldn't give them up for any price.

One of the main discomforts of Pol-e-Charkhi was the size of the cells. The dimensions were so small that inmates weren't able to stretch out full-length to sleep at night. Instead, we had to lie on our backs with our legs resting against the wall. As had been the case at *Sedarat*, having one man's legs sliding down during the night and crashing into someone else was a common occurence.

Another hardship was not so amusing. Afghan winters are bitter cold, and none of the prison cells were heated. A single blanket made of rough, khaki-colored wool comprised both bed and bedding for each prisoner. Using half the blanket to lie on, and the remaining half as a covering, we huddled together, trying to stay warm through those long winter nights.

On the positive side, Hafiz and other inmates told me that conditions in Pol-e-Charkhi had greatly improved over what they had been a few months before. The current warden's predecessor was a sadistic man who enjoyed seeing others suffer. Baiting and taunting the political prisoners was one of his favorite sports.

Then one day, an inmate nicknamed Pancheeri by the other men, took it upon himself to remedy the situation. After smuggling a knife from someone in the criminal section, Pancheeri attacked the warden and stabbed him in the stomach.

The warden survived, and Pancheeri paid for his actions with his life, but the incident served its purpose. A new warden was brought in who vowed that abuses against the political prisoners would stop. Among other things, he even promised that a library would be made available to inmates. This never happened, of course, but the gesture helped pacify the angry storm of emotions and life at Pol-e-Charkhi calmed down.

On Fridays, prisoners were permitted to have visitors who brought them money, clothes and food from the outside. The inmates were not allowed to actually see these visitors, however. Instead, they were handed a list of the various items which had been brought by family members or friends. After signing the list, the inmates gave it back to the soldiers in order to receive their supplies.

Unfortunately, no one knew that I was alive, so I never received anything from the outside. Thanks to the generosity of our cellmates, Hafiz and I were able to enjoy an occasional treat.

One of these kind souls was a young man by the name of Azimy. A short, round man, with a shy face and deeply poetic nature, Azimy was an only child. His mother frequently brought him delicious homemade food and other items. Whatever the gift might be, Azimy always shared with the rest of us.

Besides the obvious discomforts of prison life, Azimy was suffering from the pains of unrequited love. Before his arrest, he had been very much in love with a girl he'd known at the university. Azimy left Afghanistan to study in Europe for a few months, and when he returned, the young woman was engaged to someone else. Despite this fact, he still enjoyed talking about his lost love to the rest of us.

"I'm not going to tell you her name," he would say. "Just think of the most beautiful name you can imagine. She was tall and slender. Her face was like a full, shining moon and her eyes were the shape of baked almonds. Every time I looked into their liquid beauty, I could see the innocence and shyness of a beautiful little deer. Her hair was long and shiny, with dark curls that looked like thousands of black snakes wrapped around each other in perfect circles. And her lips would start the hottest fire in any man's heart .... "

One day as Azimy was describing the lady's many charms, I remembered some gossip I'd heard in college about one of our classmates who was in love with a certain young woman, but had to leave her in order to study in Europe. Suddenly, all the pieces came together and I knew the man was Azimy.

I waited for the right moment to tell him, "I know the person you're talking about." Then, whispering in his ear I said, "Her name is Khalida."

Azimy's round eyes widened. "Please don't tell anybody her name!" he begged. "Please! If you don't, I'll buy you a carton of cigarettes."

"Okay," I said, not wanting to cause him further embarrassment. "For a carton of cigarettes, I won't tell a soul." And I didn't.

* * *

During recess periods, I enjoyed visiting with Noor, Sediq, and other inmates I had known at *Sedarat*. One day Sediq asked me to come to his cell. Someone had given him a warm jacket, and he insisted on giving me back my sportcoat. I was touched that he had kept it all these months.

The best parts of my stay at Pol-e-Charkhi were the prayer times. I will never forget the feeling I had seeing thousands of people kneeling in those long prison halls, all of us facing toward the Holy City of Mecca, sharing our deepest and most sincere thoughts with the same God.

During the long hours when we were locked in our cell, we passed the time talking about memories of our past life, playing cards, and most of all, chess. The only person in our cell who knew how to play chess besides me, was Dr. Habib. Whenever the two of us were engaged in a game, this kind doctor turned into a fiercely competitive player who hated losing more than anything else. I usually won all our games, which made him even more frustrated.

Finally, in an attempt to beat me, Dr. Habib resorted to cheating. More than once, he purposely distracted my attention from the game and when I looked back at the board, one of my bishops, or a pawn would be gone.

"What happened to my bishop?" I asked.

Dr. Habib just shrugged his shoulders and replied with an innocent smile, "Oh, I took him a while back. Don't you remember?"

On one of these occasions, my brother observed the doctor's ploys with a dry smile. "Give it up, Habib," he said. "I can tell you stories about my brother and this game."

"Some other time," Habib answered with a wave of his hand, and frowned at the board.

Hafiz ignored him and continued, "Ahmad was only eight or nine, when our Dad brought home a chess board and taught us the basic moves. No one else in the family was as fascinated by the game as Ahmad. He was always begging for someone to play a game with him. And when we wouldn't, he used to play against himself, moving from one side of the board to the other." Hafiz grinned at me. "Do you remember the time our uncles came to visit and you almost beat Uncle Aziz?"

Dr. Habib gave a frustrated sigh, but my brother went on before I could discourage him.

"My uncle Aziz was a very famous chess player," he told Habib. "And once during his visit, Aziz jokingly asked my father if he'd managed to learn anything about the game of chess. My father told him no, then said his little boy was getting really good at it. 'Why don't you play a game with Ahmad?' he suggested. Uncle Aziz was insulted at the idea of playing chess with a nine-year-old. 'I don't want to play with him,' he said. 'I know. Why don't you all join together and play against me?'

"Ahmad was equally insulted by this suggestion. Our father just smiled and told his brother that he really ought to consider playing a game with Ahmad. Finally, Aziz agreed, but he was so sure of himself that he made the mistake of not paying close attention to Ahmad's moves. Aziz was confident he could beat this little boy any time he chose. They'd been playing only a few minutes, and the next thing we knew, Ahmad had taken his queen!" Hafiz chuckled as he glanced at me. "Poor Uncle Aziz! He was perspiring and so red in the face, we thought he might explode any minute. And you were so excited, you kept hopping up and down saying, 'I took his queen! I took his queen!'

"About that time, another of our uncles walked through the room and saw what was happening. Uncle Kareen knew how humiliated Aziz would be if he lost, so he 'accidentally' tossed a pillow in their direction and knocked the pieces off the board."

By now, Hafiz was laughing so hard he had to hold his sides. "I remember, you were so disappointed and angry, you started to cry," he told me.

"Well, I could have won!" I said.

"If you had, Uncle Aziz never would have forgiven you."

The other inmates joined in the laughter and gave Hafiz an encouraging slap on the back.

"And then there was the time that Ahmad won 400 *afghanis* from some poor fellow ...." he went on, as soon as the laughter died down.

"400 *afghanis!*" Azimy echoed. "How did it happen? Tell us, Hafiz!"

Dr. Habib sighed even louder and rolled his eyes.

"Hafiz ... why not wait until after the game," I suggested.

My brother just grinned at me and told the others, "One day Ahmad was going downtown to see a movie. He had ten *afghanis* in his pocket -- just enough for his movie ticket and the bus ride home. On his way to the theater, he passed by a club where a bunch of guys were gathered around two chess players. Ahmad wandered in and started watching the game. He got so interested he forgot all about the movie. One of the players was making a lot of mistakes and after he lost the game, Ahmad went up to him and said, 'You wouldn't have lost if you did this and did that.' Naturally, this made the loser very angry, to have some young kid embarrass him in front of all his friends. 'You think you're so good?' he said, 'let's see you play a game with my partner.'

"Ahmad told the man, 'Sure, I'll play with him,' but the winner refused to play without betting, and asked Ahmad how much money he had.

"When Ahmad told him he had ten *afghanis*, they all laughed.

"'I'm not going to play unless you have 50 *afghanis*, the man said. Then the man who had just lost stepped in and told his friend: 'What about playing for 100 *afghanis*? I'll pay the other 90.'"

My brother paused for a moment to give me a smile, and our cellmates leaned forward, eager to hear the rest of the tale. I smiled back and shook my head, thinking that at least this story was better than the embarrassing ones he usually told.

"Ahmad sat down to play and in a matter of minutes, he had won the game and 100 *afghanis*," Hafiz told them with pride. "But when he tried to pay back the ninety *afghanis*, the man refused to take it. He was so delighted that Ahmad had beaten his opponent, he told him to keep the money.

"Now the other guy was getting very embarrassed and mad. He told everyone that Ahmad was just lucky and challenged him to three more games at 100 *afghanis* a piece. Ahmad said, 'Sure,' and they started to play again. By now, there was a huge crowd of people gathered around to watch this young kid playing chess with an older guy. Ahmad won all three games and came home with 400 *afghanis* in his pocket instead of the ten he started out with."

Everyone laughed and clapped to show their appreciation for the story. Everyone except poor Dr. Habib.

* * *

On Fridays, we sometimes had the privilege of getting warm water to wash ourselves and our clothes. On one of these occasions, I was standing in line to get some water, with Noor just behind me. A young inmate had been given the responsibility of doling out water to the prisoners and as we waited our turn, I couldn't help noticing his rude manner and the way he yelled at everyone.

When it was my turn, the young man poured a small amount of water in the bottom of my bucket.

"Would you please pour a little more?" I asked, thinking there was something vaguely familiar about him.

"You're not the only one who wants water around here!" he shot back and started yelling at me for daring to ask for more water.

From behind, Noor suddenly spoke up. "Just a minute. Do you know who this man is?"

"No, and I don't care," the young man answered sarcastically.

Noor ignored him and went on, "This is the guy who spent three hours washing your bloody clothes when they brought you to KhAD. And now you repay him by treating him like this."

The young man's face turned red from embarrassment and shame. Grabbing my bucket, he filled it up to the top with warm water, all the while apologizing. "I'm sorry ... I didn't know. I'm very sorry."

"That's all right," I said, thinking it would be a good idea to change the subject. "What happened to you after they took you out of KhAD that day?"

"The soldiers brought me to an army hospital where I was given blood," he said. "Then the doctors operated to remove the bullets. After I recovered, they brought me here."

I smiled at him and said, "You look much better than the last time I saw you."

The young man glanced down, too ashamed to meet my eyes.

A short time later, I learned that he felt so bad about how he had acted, that he quit his job as the person in charge of water.

Reflecting on the incident made me realize once again, how a little power and position can change a person -- even if that person is only an inmate in charge of giving water to other prisoners.

* * *

About a week after my arrival, we were awakened in the middle of the night by a huge explosion. At first we thought it was an earthquake. Then, minutes later, we heard another explosion and some of the prison walls began caving in.

The inmates were locked in their cells and had no idea what was going on. All around me I could hear men yelling for help. Some were screaming. Others praying. In the fear and chaos which followed, many inmates got sick.

A half hour later, just when we thought things were calming down, a third explosion rocked the prison. Walls shook and crumbled, and the men's terrified screams echoed through the halls.

The rest of the night passed with no further interruptions, but fear and panic had left its mark. The entire place reeked of vomit and sickness.

The next morning, we learned that some of the buildings near ours had been completely destroyed and many inmates killed or injured. But as yet, none of us knew the cause or meaning of the explosions. Fear and uncertainty spread like a disease throughout the prison.

A day later, a few of us were listening to the radio during recess, when the regular broadcast was interrupted and the voice of Babrak Karmal came on the air, giving Afghans the following message:

".... *In the name of God, the compassionate, the merciful ... dear long-suffering Muslim brothers of Afghanistan, peace be upon you.*

"*Heroic men and women of the homeland ... allow me to express the deepest sympathy for the inordinate sufferings and the blood you have shed because of the imprisonment, enforced migrations, barbaric and inhuman tortures, the martyrdom and killing of tens of thousands which have taken place under Hafizullah Amin and on the direct instructions of this blood-thirsty butcher.*

"Hafizullah Amin, this agent of the CIA and spy of American imperialism, this traitor ... received his punishment at the just revolutionary tribunal of the oppressed people of Afghanistan for his satanic and devilish deeds."

Few, if any of the political prisoners who had suffered at his hands, would mourn the loss of President Amin. Still, this was shocking news. Babrak Karmal was little more than a smooth-talking puppet whose strings were pulled by party leaders in Moscow. With him as president, we all wondered what would happen to our country.

A day or two following Karmal's announcement, a soldier came to our section of the prison with a list -- not of supplies, but names. My name was among those called, along with the thirty-three others who had been transferred from KhAD headquarters to Pol-e-Charkhi barely two weeks before. We were told to get our belongings and leave with the soldier in charge. No other explanation was given.

After such a brief reunion, saying goodbye to my brother was very difficult. Neither of us could keep back the tears as we embraced each other. For all we knew, this might be our final farewell.

In fearful silence, we followed the soldier down the long hallways and to an outer courtyard, where I was surprised to see a bus waiting instead of the windowless van which had carried us to Pol-e-Charkhi. A flicker of hope warmed my heart. Another positive sign was the fact that none of us were handcuffed, and there was only one soldier on the bus, along with the driver.

My hopes rose even higher when the bus drove away from Pol-e-Charkhi and took the road leading north to Kabul.

Then the soldier in charge stood up to announce our destination. His words struck me in the chest like a physical blow.

We were being taken back to KhAD headquarters in *Sedarat*.

Chapter 18

NIGHTMARE MEMORIES OF pain and torture flashed through my brain and I knew I would rather die than return to *Sedarat's* living hell.

Unaware of the devastating effect his words had had, the soldier went on to explain that upon our arrival at KhAD, we would be given certain forms to fill out and sign, after which we would be released.

After so many disappointments and the long months of imprisonment, it was difficult to believe this was really happening -- that the doors of the cage were opening at last.

During the journey back to Kabul, all everyone could talk about was our impending release. Would it really happen? And why were the soldiers doing this? The general consensus among the men was that it must be some kind of mollifying gesture on the part of Babrak Karmal's new regime. The reason didn't really matter. Only our freedom. Excitement brightened everyone's voices and the light of hope transformed winter's bleak landscape into scenes that were fresh and beautiful.

We were still a few miles outside of Kabul when the bus stopped in front of a large barracade. Looking out the window, I saw Russian soldiers and tanks everywhere. After a few tense moments, we were given permission to pass. We had traveled a few more miles when I saw another barracade blocking the road ahead, with more Russians all around.

I turned to Jan Mohammad, who was sitting next to me and said, "They've invaded us."

For a brief time, thoughts of freedom had filled us with happiness and excitement. What we didn't realize then was that our prison just got bigger. Now the entire country was a prison.

We arrived at *Sedarat* in late afternoon. Just being in that place again made everyone tense and nervous. Soldiers took us to a small room where we were told to wait for some officials who would come speak to us.

The instructions sounded all too familiar and as afternoon lengthened into evening, our fears and nervousness increased. Had the officials changed their minds? What if they were lying all along and had no intention of letting us go.

Around seven-thirty p.m., some "puppet" officials of the Russians finally showed up. One of these "dried asses" as the prisoners were fond of calling them, proceeded to give us a long, boring speech about patriotism and faithfulness to the new government. When he finished, we were given some documents to fill out and sign.

Then, about an hour before curfew, a soldier ushered us out of the room and to the main exit. At the door, an armed guard checked our "promise slips," and suddenly, we were out on the street.

The winter night was dark and cold, but the exhilerating air of freedom was blowing all around us. We were giddy with happiness and the incredible emotions of release. The first thing on everyone's mind was to get as far away from that place as possible. Laughing and shouting, we ran across the street. We didn't stop running until we we had put several blocks between us and *Sedarat*. Then, feeling reasonably safe, we stopped to embrace each other and say our goodbyes.

I invited Jan Mohammad to come to my house since his home was in another province several hundred miles away. We whistled for a cab, and were on our way.

Jan Mohammad were like excited children, laughing and talking and telling the driver all about our release from prison. Seeing the familiar sites of Kabul was a totally new experience for me, because I was seeing these places with new eyes.

When the cab stopped in front of the lane leading to my house, I asked the driver to please wait while I went inside to get some money to pay him.

"Don't worry guys!" he told us with a big grin. "This one's on me."

Jan Mohammad and I were so happy, we couldn't stop ourselves from hugging the driver. He got back in the cab with a big grin on his face, and gave us a friendly salute before driving away.

The house I had left on that summer day nearly seven months before, stood dark and silent against the black mountainside. I was shaking with happiness and anticipation more than the cold, as Jan Mohammad and I climbed the frosty steps and walked across the moonlit courtyard. Once inside, I invited my friend to wait in the hall while I searched for my family.

The living room was dark and empty. So were the bedrooms. I had a few unsettling moments, wondering where everyone was.

Then, walking back to the front hall, I saw the dark silhouette of a man outside on the terrace. As my eyes adjusted to the darkness, I recognized my friend Iqbal. He was standing alone, enjoying the beauty of the moon and the cold brilliance of the winter sky.

Iqbal and I had known each other for years. We loved the same kind of music, we studied together and often enjoyed a game of chess. Silently, I approached my friend from behind, then covered his eyes with my hands.

"Don't play games, Zoor," he said, thinking I was my older brother. "I'm not in the mood."

I smiled and said nothing.

Iqbal stiffened, suddenly realizing the person holding his eyes was not Zoor. He turned around and stared at me as if I were a ghost, then grabbed my arms.

"My God, it's you! We all thought you were dead!"

"I know, but I'm alive -- and I'm free!" I told him joyfully.

After we had embraced, I asked him where my family was.

"I'll take you to them," he offered. "They're all in the room with the stove."

I was so excited to see my family again, I'd forgotten that in the wintertime it was too expensive to heat all the rooms.

With my heart in my throat, I opened the door to the small room where my family was gathered.

There was a brief moment of silence, while I looked into their beautiful faces, then everyone burst out with the same words: "Oh, my God, it's Ahmad!"

Those simple words were spoken in such amazed and shocked tones that my mind and pen are not capable of describing it. My mother's emotions were like a little child who pounds his feet on the ground to show his excitement. Her fingers were unconsciously pulling at her hair as tears ran down her cheeks. "My baby ... my baby," she repeated again and again.

I went to her and held her in my arms, pressing her hard against me, as if I were squeezing all of the love that I had missed during the time of my imprisonment.

Soon I felt the arms of my entire family around me. My sisters. My brothers. And my father.

When I asked about my wife and son, Shaima explained that Zarghuna and Jossef were visiting some relatives. Without a word, Habib, who was a cab driver, left to go get them.

After our emotions had calmed a little, I invited Jan Mohammad to come inside and meet my family. They gave him a warm welcome and my sisters quickly offered to get the guest room ready for him.

Taking my first hot shower in over seven months was an experience of pure joy for all my senses. The next thing Jan Mohammad and I did was burn our clothes, with the exception of my sport coat, which I wanted to keep as a reminder of the lessons I had learned in prison.

By the time Habib returned with my wife and son, I was looking a little more presentable. In Afghanistan, family members greet each other with excitement and emotion, but it is not considered proper behavior for husbands and wives to show their affection in public. Zarghuna came toward me with shining eyes, and we kissed one other on each cheek as was customary.

Jossef wasn't sure he liked this thin, ragged stranger who had been his father. When I tried to take him in my arms, he pulled away and started to cry. No matter what I said or did, he kept crying and refused to come to me.

Despite this momentary awkwardness, my heart was full. I cannot imagine greater happiness than the emotions I felt at seeing my wife and son again.

That night, so much that had been lost was returned to me. My home. My family. A clean, soft bed. And the blessing of a woman's love.

* * *

Early the next morning, I was awakened by the soft touch of someone's fingers on my face. I opened bleary eyes and discovered Jossef standing by my bed with the cutest smile on his chubby round face. This time he didn't object when I took him in my arms, and put him next to me in the bed. He was talking like a little bird with a beautiful childish accent. In those moments, I realized that it was worth all the pain and humiliation I had gone through to be welcomed in the arms of this innocent child.

It was still early enough that most of the family was still sleeping. Leaving Jossef with his mother, I got up and went into the hall. From the next room, I could hear the familiar sound of my father reading outloud from the Holy Koran. I stood outside the room for a moment to listen. I could feel the joy and gratitude pouring from his voice, as if he were savoring all the sweetness of the fruits that the seeds of his honest belief and deep prayers had sown.

When I entered the room, I saw my father sitting on the floor with the Holy Koran in front of him on a pillow. He sensed my presence but went on reading, his body rocking back and forth in a familiar rhythm. I sat down in the corner, content to watch his fascinating, wrinkled face that was decorated with a beautiful smile of deep concentration.

After reading aloud for another five minutes or so, he closed the book and put it on the top shelf of the closet. When he turned to look at me, tears of joy were running down my cheeks. My father came closer and put a hand on the back of my neck, giving me an affectionate shake. Then he, too, lost control of his emotions and turned away.

I knew he was crying, and out of embarrassment, I left the room, missing the perfect opportunity to tell my father how much I loved him.

Outside in the courtyard, I found Jan Mohammad sitting on the steps, enjoying an early morning cigarette and staring at the sky.

"It's not square any more," I said.

He nodded and said simply, "It's beautiful."

After breakfast, my father loaned me some money to give Jan Mohammad for his trip home and I walked my friend to the bus stop. In my mind, I can still see his smiling face in the back window as he waved goodbye, while the bus got smaller and smaller in the distance.

The rest of the day, I spent with my family. I was grateful to learn that Mina and Farid and their new little daughter were safe In spite of the fact they were still in hiding, everyone assured me that Mina would manage a visit as soon as she learned of our release. Zoor was in Pakistan at the moment, and Shaima was teaching algebra and chemistry at a local high school. A happy surprise was the news that my sister Rahella had married Anwar, a good friend of the family, some months before. They were living in Iran where Anwar was a surgeon in a large hospital. I was thrilled and amazed to know that my beautiful younger sister was expecting a baby. The three youngest in the family -- Zhora, Fahima and Rahim -- were still attending school, although changes in the government and the recent invasion often disrupted their schedules.

Details of the invasion itself were still sketchy, but from everything I was told, the outlook for Afghanistan's future was grim. Radio and television broadcasts were controlled by the Communists, but occasionally, my family was able to receive some uncensored news from the rebel station in Peshawar, or P.R.I. According to these sources, the first Soviet heavy transport planes had rumbled into Kabul airport on December 24th and within three days, the city of Kabul was in their hands. Two of the three telephone exchanges in the capital had been blown up by Soviet demolition teams, and *Sedarat* itself had been stormed by troops of the 105th Division. On December 27, a special KGB hit team, supported by Soviet airborne commanders, attacked Darulaman Palace where Amin had barracaded himself.

On the morning of December 28th, the official Afghan broadcasting network announced President Amin's overthrow, saying he had been tried and found guilty by a "revolutionary Tribunal," and executed for his "crimes against the people."

I thought back to that terrifying night at Pol-e-Charkhi when explosions had rocked the prison. That must have been the beginning of the invasion, and the night Amin was killed. Bombing the prison had been just another show of force and power by the invading Soviet army.

It would have taken much more than a Russian invasion to dampen my family's spirits that day. My mother was so happy, I'm sure the amount of food she cooked for us could have fed an entire army. Being together was such a beautiful miracle, that no one wanted to add any unpleasantness to the day by asking me about my experiences in *Sedarat*. I, too, wanted to put the horrors of that time behind me.

But that night, in the quiet of my room, sleep refused to come. Every time I started to drift off, the old familiar nightmares were there, hovering like black birds of prey on the edge of my consciousness ....

I wasn't sure how to begin, but I desperately needed to talk about what had happened. When I broached the subject to my wife, she told me not to say anything about it and advised me to just forgot about the whole thing.

The rest of the night, I lay awake, staring at the ceiling, fighting my demons in lonely silence.

The next morning, I decided to leave the house and take a bus into the city. All that day I rode one bus after another, getting off to visit my favorite places -- the soccer field and the chess club at *Shari Noh,* the New City Park. I went to my school, to theaters and the beautiful tree-lined walks where young men and women were fond of meeting. My appreciation for these places was greater than ever before, yet it was impossible to fully enjoy them because of all the changes.

Everywhere I went, there were KhAD agents and Russian soldiers. I was free, but I didn't feel free. It seemed as if the entire city was invaded by dark clouds of distrust, sadness and fear.

I was boarding a bus to return home, when I noticed a familiar face toward the back. It was Quassim! I was overjoyed to know that he was still alive, and realized from his expression that he recognized me. Before I could make my way down the aisle, Quassim looked away and quickly got off the bus.

The incident left me with a very uneasy feeling. The look between us had lasted no more than a few seconds, but it was long enough to see the fear in his eyes. And something else that disturbed me even more. Guilt.

My thoughts were deep and heavy during the remainder of the ride. The experience with Quassim left me feeling so discouraged that I now doubted the wisdom of seeking out any of my other friends.

Walking up the long lane to my home, I learned there had been many changes in our immediate neighborhood, as well as the city. When I asked people where certain friends or neighbors were, their answers filled me with sadness. Some had been arrested and executed, many had fled the country, and others simply disappeared.

That evening, I brought up the situation with my family, and they confirmed what the neighbors had said. Members of the secret police were going into movie theaters, bazaars and other public places and taking away the young men. And there had been several instances where men who had been freed from prison, like myself, were rearrested and taken back to KhAD.

Fear and uncertainty, like the menacing presence of Russian soldiers, were everywhere.

A week following my release, the government announced that it was going to pardon all the political prisoners at Pol-e-Charkhi. Everyone knew this was a political move by Babrak Karmal and the Russians to get public support for their new regime, but the gesture offered hope to families like ours, who still had loved ones in prison.

When the appointed day arrived, I took a bus to the prison and waited outside the massive gates. Many buses and other vehicles were already there lining the roadway, along with thousands of people eagerly waiting to see their loved ones. The mood of the crowd was full of hope, excitement and anticipation.

Finally, the moment arrived and the prison doors opened. My eyes filled with tears as I watched the inmates exit in single file, making their way through the throngs of people who were lined up on either side. Approximately two hundred men had come out of the prison when I saw my brother's smiling face.

After a joyful reunion, Hafiz and I both wanted to stay until the rest of the prisoners had been released. I'm not sure of the exact number who were freed that day, but it couldn't have been more than a thousand. Soldiers and the secret police arrested at least two to three times that amount every week.

When the last man had come out, the iron gates closed and gray dust began rising from the ground to the sky above, like the people's tears all around me.

I have no words to express all the sorrow behind the disappointed eyes of children who had waited in vain for their fathers, wives for their husbands, and mothers for their sons. I can only say that instead of a time of celebration, that bitter January day became a time of national mourning.

The pain and injustice of that scene helped me make up my mind. As much as I loved my country, I knew I couldn't stay in Afghanistan any longer. I was fooling myself if I thought the chances of being arrested again were only a threat. Considering how much I knew about *Sedarat* and the members of KhAD, it was only a matter of time.

Chapter 19

THE BUS RIDE back to Kabul was a silent one. When I shared my decision to leave the country with Hafiz, he said without hesitation that he wanted to go with me. But how or when this would happen, neither of us knew.

A day or two after my brother's release from prison, my sister Mina came to our home to visit us. To avoid recognition by the Russians and KhAD agents, she arrived wearing a *chadiri*. Safely inside the house, she removed the long Afghan veil that covered her face and body.

I will never forget that moment when she first saw me. Mina ran forward and kissed my hands, my neck, and my face. All the while, she was sobbing and telling me how horrible it had been for her to see the list of people who were condemned to death while I was in prison, never knowing what had happened to me.

I held my sister in my arms, trying to comfort her and wipe away her tears with my hand, even though many of my own were falling.

When she regained her composure, there were a few moments of silence between us. I think she must have sensed what I needed to tell her. Mina accepted our decision to leave the country with the quiet courage and strength that I have always loved in her.

"In a few days, I'll arrange a meeting for you and Hafiz with Farid," she told me. "He's been very anxious to see you, and I know he'll want to help you escape."

During the days which followed, I found myself saying silent goodbyes to people and places that I loved. And there was still a painful promise that I needed to keep to a friend.

One morning, without mentioning to my family where I was going, I put Ibrahim's sweater in a paper bag and took a bus to the apartment where he had lived. I had no difficulty finding the address, as one of my uncles lived in the same complex.

During the bus ride downtown, I was determined to keep my thoughts positive, and concentrated on picturing my friend's surprised face when he opened the door and discovered I was still alive.

Not until I was approaching the huge Russian-built apartment complex, did my optimism start to falter. By the time I was standing in front of Ibrahim's door, my palms were sweating and I no longer knew whether it was anticipation or fear that quickened my breathing.

A young girl with big brown eyes answered my knock. She looked so much like Ibrahim, I knew immediately this must be the little sister he had talked so much about. It was all I could do not to pick her up and hug her in my arms. Instead, I smiled down at her and asked if there was an adult at home. Without saying a word, she shut the door and called out someone's name. Moments later, the door was opened by a pretty woman in her early twenties. She wasn't wearing any makeup, and her eyes were red and puffy as if she had been crying recently. Looking at her long, dark hair, I could tell that it hadn't been brushed in a long time.

"My name is Ahmad," I said. "I'm a friend of Ibrahim's, and I haven't seen him in a long time. How is he?"

The young woman seemed very nervous and emotionally fragile, but as soon as she heard her husband's name, she gave me a sad smile. Blinking back the tears, she invited me to come in.

The apartment was humbly furnished with a few pictures of her and Ibrahim hanging on the walls. I went closer to one of the pictures and stared at his smiling face. In my mind, I could still hear him humming those simple tunes whenever he was thinking of his past. They might even have been the same tunes that he once hummed to this beautiful lady I was with right now.

Ibrahim's wife had no way of knowing my thoughts or that I was the last person he had spoken to about her, telling me how much he truly loved and missed her. The more this painful stream of memories circulated through my thoughts, the more nervous I became.

When this fragile young woman found out that the message of Ibrahim's last destination was in the paper bag I clutched in my hands, what would she do? Seeing her present emotional state, I was afraid she wouldn't be able to deal with it.

In a moment, my mind was made up. I didn't want to be the white camel, or the messenger of death, as they say in my country.

We talked for a few more minutes, then I left the apartment, still holding the bag with Ibrahim's blue sweater. All the way home, I wondered if I'd done the right thing. Right or wrong, I knew I couldn't crush the small blossom of hope that she might still be cherishing for her husband's return.

* * *

Out of all my friends, Zia and Samad were the only ones who had the courage to visit my family during my imprisonment. During those final days in Kabul, I spent a memorable night at each of their homes, grateful to see their faces and enjoy the warmth of our friendship one last time.

When I arrived at Zia's house, everyone in his family gathered around me with curious questions about my ordeal. Before I could say a word, Zia interrupted to ask if I'd heard about his sister's recent marriage.

I shook my head, sensing an unspoken warning in my friend's eyes and voice. He went on to tell me a little about the wedding and the fact that his sister's new husband was one of the Investigators at KhAD.

I offered my congratulations on her marriage, and for the rest of the evening, carefully omitted saying anything about *Sedarat* and its Investigators.

The night spent at Samad's home was much easier on my nerves. Bismilah, Zia and another college friend by the name of Noor Aga, were already there, waiting to see me. The five of us played cards and talked all night long. They knew that my present situation was very uncertain and wondered what I was going to do. I felt safe in confiding to them that Hafiz and I were going to try to escape.

"What about your college diploma?" Noor Aga asked, knowing how much it meant to me.

I explained that I was arrested before I could finish my thesis, so I would just have to leave the country without it. Then Noor Aga told me that one of his cousins knew a lot of people in the department where they prepared diplomas for the University.

"Perhaps he could do something for you," he suggested. "I'll see if I can make arrangements for you to meet him."

True to his word, the very next day I had an appointment with my friend's cousin. The man was very understanding and said he'd like to help me, but admitted he'd never done anything like this before. The most difficult part of getting my diploma would be acquiring the proper signatures with the stamp of the Minister of Higher Education.

"I'm not sure what I can do for you," he said finally, "but I'll try my best. Come back in a couple of days."

When I returned to his office two days later, the man greeted me politely, then said in a low tone, "Meet me in one hour at the bus station."

To fill the time until then, I walked around the campus, trying to absorb a few more details from this beautiful place where I had drawn the blueprints of so many unfinished dreams. The tall trees on either side of the streets were stark and bare, unlike the leafy canopies I had walked along in spring and summer. I passed the building where I had taken all my French classes ... the theater, and the secluded spots where young men and women would "accidentally" meet and talk.

Now, all these scenes must be placed in the archives of memory.

I made my way to the bus station at the appointed time, and moments later, saw Noor Aga's cousin approaching me through the crowd. Under one arm, he carried a thick book with a manilla folder tucked inside.

"Come take a walk with me," he said, for the benefit of anyone who might be listening.

I fell into step beside him and as we walked, he told me that he'd risked this dangerous act, not merely as a favor to his cousin, but because he hated the present government.

Then, removing the folder from the book, he handed me my college diploma. "Don't tell a soul about this," he cautioned. "If you do, it will be my death sentence."

I looked at the document, then at my friend's cousin, hoping my grateful eyes would convey at least part of my feelings. After waiting so long for this moment, mere words seemed sadly inadequate to express my thanks.

During the bus ride home, I sat staring at the symbol of all those years of education ... my picture, and the official signatures and stamp of the University of Kabul. Under ordinary circumstances, I probably would have been jumping up and down from excitement. Now, my emotions were mixed and my mood sober.

I remembered the day I'd brought home my high school diploma. Everyone was so happy and proud. Now, even though I was the first person in my family to receive a college degree, I was denied the satisfaction of seeing the joy on their faces and the tears of pride shining in my father's eyes.

In my mind, I suddenly saw another pair of eyes, and a single tear slipping down a nameless young man's tortured face. My perspective shifted from thoughts of self pity to a realization that in many ways, the "education" I received at *Sedarat* was equally as valuable as the one from the University of Kabul.

Very carefully, I slipped the document back inside its folder.

When I arrived home, Hafiz met me with the news that Mina had come by while I was out, and given him the address where we were to meet Farid the next day.

So much was happening in such a short time, that once again, although I was exhausted from the day's events, sleep refused to come. Lying in bed next to my wife, I felt the horrors of *Sedarat* pressing ever closer. Desperate to push them away, I made a second attempt to talk with Zarghuna about my experiences there. Once again, she stopped me before I had a chance to begin, saying she didn't want to hear about those sad stories.

"You need to forget that place and never bring up the subject again," she told me.

I didn't blame her for reacting that way, but suddenly, I felt as if she had built a huge wall between us. All night long, I lay staring at the ceiling, smoking one cigarette after another, and thinking. If my own wife didn't want to know what had happened to me, it would probably be best if I said nothing about it to the rest of the family.

Somehow, I would have to find a way to deal with the nightmares and the memories by myself.

* * *

Late the following afternoon, Hafiz and I arrived at the address Mina had given us. A polite man in his late thirties, answered our knock.

"May I have your names, please?" he asked. After telling him, the man nodded. "This way, please."

We were taken to a guest room not far from the entry. After making sure that Hafiz and I were comfortably seated on a mattress, the man excused himself. Minutes later, he returned, bringing us cookies and tea.

As we drank the tea, he made polite conversation, asking which school we had attended and what kind of jobs we had. It was getting dark when we heard a knock on the door. Our host left to answer it, and came back accompanied by a tall man wearing a turban and a long *chapan*. Not until he removed the coat and was unwinding the turban did I recognize him. It was Farid!

My brother-in-law had shaved his mustache and beard and cut his hair very short. Farid looked so different, I still had difficulty believing it was really him.

After embracing, the three of us sat down together and started to laugh. I'm sure some of that laughter stemmed from the pure happiness of seeing each other again, but a good part of it came from the release of tense emotion. It was amazing to think that all three of us had been arrested, tortured, and imprisoned -- yet, now at this very moment, we were alive and gathered under the same roof.

Farid and I had known each other for years, yet there was much about his life that remained a mystery. I did know he was the youngest child in his family. Farid's father was a very rich man who owned a lot of land in different provinces of Afghanistan. When Farid was a young boy, most of his friends were the children of poor peasants who worked for his father. Seeing the difference between the peasants' humble lifestyle, and all the comforts and possessions of his father, made a deep impression on him. This disparity between the rich and the poor created a big conflict for Farid over the years -- first between him and his father, and later, between Farid and the system.

He was determined to improve conditions for the poor and bring about changes in Afghan society. In addition to becoming a doctor, he also became involved in politics. I never doubted his love for Mina and members of our family, but when it came to politics, Farid was a very secretive man. There was much about him that I would probably never know, but now, seeing him again after all these months, my curiosity on one point demanded an answer.

"How did you escape?" I asked him.

"Do you remember the night when they were taking you to the bathroom, and I asked you if Mina had had a boy or a girl?" he said.

"How could I ever forget that night?"

Farid's eyes met mine in sympathetic understanding. "That night I was feeling very weak, mentally as well as from the torture. I knew the next time they took me, they could break me down, so I decided to commit suicide before that happened. Early the next morning while it was still dark, I asked the soldier who was on duty walking the halls, to take me outside to the latrine. When I was inside the stall, I took off my shirt and planned to hang myself from one of the beams in the roof. Fortunately, about that time, someone came by and called to the soldier who was waiting for me. He told me to wait inside and said he'd be back soon.

"As soon as he was gone, I reached for the wooden beam and started wrapping my shirt around it. Then I noticed the board was loose. I pushed it up and down a few times and after a minute, took out the entire beam. This left a big hole in the roof, which was old anyway, and partly ruined by the weather. I had nothing to lose, so I climbed through the hole onto the roof. Do you remember that high wall behind the latrine?" he asked us, and went on after our nod. "I couldn't see anyone on the other side, so I jumped down to the courtyard and hid behind one of the trees. For a second, I wasn't sure what to do, because the courtyard was surrounded by walls like all the others. Then I noticed one of the larger trees grew very close to the wall. All I had to do was climb the tree, get on the wall and jump down to the other side. And there I was on the main road outside the prison. I couldn't believe it! What about you and Hafiz?" he wanted to know. "Tell me what happened to you after I escaped."

Not wanting him to feel too bad, I gave him a condensed version of my torture, then told him about the friends of his that I'd met during my time in *Sedarat*. Farid listened intently, tears filling his eyes.

When I finished speaking, the three of us sat in contemplative silence for a long moment. Then Farid took a stack of money out of his pocket. "I brought you 10,000 *afghanis*. It might not be enough for you to go to Iran, but it's all I could arrange right now. The good news is, Anwar and Rahella are there and I think they might be able to help you."

Farid looked at me, and his voice tightened with emotion. "I'm sorry that you had to go through so much because of me."

"It's a good thing I didn't know anything about your party or your friends," I told him frankly. "Being under so much torture, I probably would have told the Investigators everything."

Farid nodded without speaking, then invited us to spend the night at his friend's house.

Much of the time was spent just talking together. I think we all realized this might be our last time together.

The next morning after breakfast, with tears and embraces, we said our goodbyes. In each of our hearts was the prayer that someday, *in Shala,* God willing, we would meet again in better times.

Before returning home, Hafiz and I used part of the money Farid had given us to buy plane tickets for Herat. We both agreed it would be wise not to tell the family the exact day we were leaving. Besides wanting to spare them the trauma and worry, it was vital to their safety and ours. Some of our neighbors were Communists, and if one of them happened to learn that Hafiz and I were going to leave the country, we were certain to be arrested.

The only person who knew about our plans was a neighbor and friend by the name of Homayoon. In addition to being a trusted friend, Homayoon was also a flight engineer at the Kabul airport. Knowing this, I made a point of asking him what we could take with us on the plane without arousing any suspicion. Homayoon said that officials at the airport were searching everything -- people's bags and their clothes. There were even body searches.

I told him that I wanted to take my high school and college diplomas with me, but had some concerns that this might look suspicious to the airport security.

"Don't worry," my friend said. "I know almost everyone at the airport. I'll be glad to care of it for you. Just give me the documents and I'll make sure you get them after you arrive in Herat."

The day before our plane was scheduled to leave, I took a bus downtown to see one of my cousins. There weren't many people in the bus and glancing down the aisle, I noticed an older man sitting alone next to a window. It was Arjung!

For a split second, the painful experience with Quassim made me hesitate, then I hurried down the aisle.

Arjung was staring intently out the window. God only knows what he was thinking, because he didn't look up or notice me as I sat down beside him.

Putting a hand on his knee, I said, "How are you, Arjung?"

The man stared at me with unbelieving eyes. Then he jumped up and grabbed me in his arms. "Oh my God, you're alive! Why didn't you come to see me?"

I told him how discouraged I was about visiting anyone I'd known in *Sedarat* after meeting Quassim. Arjung just looked at me with those wonderful, compassionate eyes, then embraced me again.

My original plans were set aside, when Arjung insisted on taking me to his place of business. There, I met his children and they cooked us a wonderful meal.

Arjung and I spent the rest of the day talking about our time in KhAD, the men we had known, and how our releases had come about. Sharing the pain and the memories, the weight of my burden began to lessen. Here at last, was someone who knew and understood. When Arjung asked about my plans for the future, I told him that I was leaving the country the next day.

Neither of us could believe how incredible it was that we should meet on my last day in Kabul.

Our parting was not without tears, but, as I had told him that day in prison, at least we had the chance to say our last goodbyes.

Early the next morning, I stood beside my son's bed, looking down at his peacefully sleeping face. I bent over him, unable to stop myself from kissing his face, his hands, and his chubby feet. Jossef woke up and I picked him up, hushing him in my arms for a few minutes until he went back to sleep. Then, with tears streaming down my face, I laid him back in his bed and left the room.

Everyone in my family was still sleeping, except my father. When Hafiz and I entered the room, he closed the Holy Book and took both of us into his arms. The three of us stood there, holding each other and crying unashamedly like little babies.

Then, taking the Koran in his hands, he held the book high enough for us to stand beneath it, and said through his tears, "May *Allah* and this book protect you, my sons."

I left my home in the chill of a winter dawn, not knowing this would be the last time I ever saw or spoke to him.

Chapter 20

HAFIZ AND I arrived at the Kabul airport nearly an hour before our scheduled departure time of eight a.m. Minutes later, it was announced that the flight to Herat would be delayed three hours for mechanical reasons. This news was more than disheartening. Glancing around the terminal, I realized the next few hours would be very tense and potentially dangerous for me.

At *Sedarat,* the Investigators were divided into two groups -- those who made arrests and those in charge of interrogation and torture. I was most familiar with those over torture, but I knew many Investigators from the first group by name as well as sight. Standing by a door just yards away, was one of the KhAD agents assigned to making arrests.

"There are lots of dogs searching for bones here," I told Hafiz, "and I am a very greasy target. They all know that I know them. I think it would be best if you stayed away from me. I'm going to sit at the end of the hall. Don't come over to me or talk to me."

Hafiz and I parted company, and moments after I sat down, one of the Investigators walked past. Then another. Then a third. After that I lost count, but there must have been at least a dozen or more agents in the airport terminal that morning and nearly every one of them managed to walk down the hall where I was sitting. Some of the men gave me a dirty look as they passed by. Others sent me a poisonous smile.

I was glancing around, trying to decide where I should go, when one of the Investigators approached me and said, "They let you go, huh?"

"Yes, sir," I answered, hoping he wouldn't notice how my voice was shaking.

The man had no idea how much I despised his presence. How much I hated his voice, and how much I detested his shiny shoes and his stolen suit.

"Where are you going?" he asked, sitting down in the chair next to mine.

For a moment, I didn't know what to say. Then I told him, "I have a sister living in Herat. She's very sick and I haven't seen her in a long time."

The Investigator shook his head and made an awful sound with his trumpet-looking nose. "Mmmm...."

I knew he was going to interrogate me further. My mind was running as fast as it could to find an excuse to end this conversation. The only thing I could come up with was, "Do you have a cigarette, sir?"

He shook his head again. "I don't smoke."

I shrugged nervously and asked, "Do you know where I could buy a pack around here?"

"No, I don't. Maybe you should ask a smoker."

"That's a good idea," I agreed. "I'm going to do that. It was nice meeting you, sir."

I got up and walked away without any particular destination in mind. Looking over my shoulder a moment later, I saw the man had gone. A sense of urgency throbbing inside me insisted that I had better be out of sight before he returned.

The men's restroom was only a few feet away, and right then, that seemed as good a place as any. Walking toward the restroom, I noticed Hafiz coming up the stairs and motioned for him to follow me.

Wash basins lined one wall of the room, with an equal amount of toilets on the other. I made a quick check of the floor beneath the stalls, and felt a little better knowing I was the room's only occupant.

Hafiz entered seconds later, looking as nervous as I felt. I briefly told him what had happened with the Investigator, and said, "I know they're going to arrest me again, because they're afraid of being recognized. I'm going to stay in here until our plane leaves. Don't come to get me until the last minute. It might look suspicious if they see you coming and going."

Hafiz was reluctant to leave me, but under the circumstances, agreed that it was the safest course of action. After he had gone, I went into the last stall on the end, shut the door and sat down cross-legged on the toilet seat. Spending a couple of hours in the bathroom wouldn't be so bad, I told myself. Compared to the months at *Sedarat*, this would be a 'glass of water.'

Minutes crawled by. I read and reread the various messages people had scribbled on the door and the walls. Some were crude. Others were swear words and curses against the government and various Communist leaders, especially Brezhnev, who was referred to as the "cruel fat pig." One joke that made me laugh in spite of myself was: *Who has the longest road to get to the bathroom? Babrak Karmal, because every time he needs to use it, he has to go to Moscow.*

From my position, all I could see of the other occupants who used the restroom was their feet. Whenever a man with shiny shoes entered one of the stalls, I felt myself starting to panic, and tried to hold my breath until he had gone. I especially dreaded the thought of seeing the same pair of shoes twice, afraid the owner might be returning because he suspected this was where I was hiding.

Even if the Investigators had no intention of arresting me, the fear was there. Yet along with the anxiety, there were comic moments as well.

When people think they are alone in the bathroom, they do some strange things. After letting go of all the humanly possible body noises, they make incredible sounds of satisfaction, as if they were having an orgasm. Other times, they talk to themselves and say weird things.

Aside from the fear, the most unpleasant part of my adventure in the bathroom was putting up with the pungent natural perfume that changed every five minutes or so as different men came in to use the toilet. Right when I was beginning to get used to one smell, someone else would come in. There were times I couldn't help wondering what on earth these people had for breakfast.

There isn't much a person can do to entertain himself in such unusual circumstances. It would have been easier if I'd had a deck of cards, or even a pen, so I could add a few sayings of my own to the walls. Since I didn't, I tried to keep my mind on other things. It was next to impossible trying to imagine anything pleasant when I was so often interrupted by others' bodily functions.

One minute I was bored. The next I was terrified. God knows how much I wanted to whistle a tune, but there was always the chance that the next person coming in might hear me. Sometimes, when I was certain I was alone, I would start singing in a low voice, barely loud enough for me to hear. Then as soon as someone entered, I would carry the tune in my mind.

My worst fear was that one of the Investigators would open the door of the last stall and find me. As time went on, that fear grew larger and larger. No matter how hard I tried to shove it away, the thought never left my mind. I knew what these men were capable of and what would happen if I were arrested again.

Finally, I put my elbows on my crossed legs, and covered my face with my hands. In a small way, this gave me the feeling of being alone in the dark, somewhere far away from all this madness. Sitting there in despair, the thought came into my mind that I needed to ask God for help.

Oh, dear God ... I pleaded. *Let them kill me! Take my life if you want to. But please ... don't let them take me back to that horrible place alive!*

I was drowning in these thoughts when I heard my brother's anxious whisper. "Ahmad, are you still there?"

"Yes," I answered. "I told you not to come here."

"I know, but I'm worried about you."

"I'm fine, Hafiz. Please go away. Just come and get me when it's time ... please," I pleaded.

"All right, but I thought you might want something to drink. Here." He handed me a bottled soft drink, then left.

When the time finally arrived for our flight to leave, my legs were so stiff and cramped from sitting on the toilet, I could hardly walk. Fortunately, the concourse was crowded with lots of other people as Hafiz and I made our way to the gate. Every time I noticed an agent from KhAD, I kept on walking and forced myself to look straight ahead as if I hadn't seen them.

The plane was well on its way to Herat, before was I able to relax. Then, I began describing my experience in the bathroom to Hafiz. Listening to me, his mouth twitched into a smile. I knew my brother felt genuinely sorry for me, but he couldn't stop himself from laughing.

Now that it was over, neither could I. Laughter released the final cords of tension and I leaned back to look out the window at an endless stretch of sky. Herat was only a few hours away. And from there ... freedom.

* * *

As our plane approached the outskirts of the city, Hafiz and I were confronted with a disturbing sight below.

Russian tanks, planes, and military equipment were everywhere. Hafiz pointed out some of the most sophisticated MIG fighters as well as heavy transports. Suddenly, Herat didn't seem as far away from the Russians after all.

When the plane landed, my concerns shifted from the obvious signs of the Soviet military to something more personal. My friend Homayoon had promised that his contact at the Kabul airport would get my diplomas to me, but as yet, I didn't know who that contact was or how this would take place.

Hafiz and I were among the last passengers to exit the plane. As we made our way down the narrow aisle, the pilot approached and asked my name. For a wild moment, I wondered if he might be a KhAD agent. I answered his question in a dry voice.

Without a word, he reached into the inside pocket of his jacket and took out my diplomas.

"I believe these are yours," he said, handing them to me.

"Yes ... they are. Thank you very much."

He nodded politely, then said in a low tone, "Don't mention this to anyone," and walked away.

Hafiz and I had only a single suitcase each, and experienced no difficulties leaving the airport. In minutes, we had found a cab and were on our way to the home of Anwar's oldest brother, Omar.

Omar himself met us at the door. It had been several years since I had last seen this good friend of the family, but the warmth of our meeting was tempered by the unsettling news that Omar's house had been under surveillance for the past several days. After ushering us inside, he strongly cautioned us not to leave the house until all the arrangements for our escape had been made. Not wanting to endanger our host or ourselves, we readily agreed.

Omar's home was large and beautifully furnished, but even such pleasant surroundings couldn't prevent the uncomfortable feeling that once again, I was in prison.

That evening after dinner, my brother and I sat in the living room, drinking tea and talking with our host and his two younger brothers, Zaher and Taher.

Zaher was a good-looking man in his mid-twenties, about six feet tall with a thin mustache and pale skin. He was very fond of stylish European clothes and always meticulously groomed -- especially where his hair was concerned.

Taher was a year or so younger, with darker skin and small black eyes that looked even smaller when he smiled, which he did often. Like his older brother, Taher's wavy dark hair was also well-groomed and shiny. The motive for this had more to do with fear than grooming habits. Ever since their two older brothers, Iqbal and Anwar had begun losing some of their hair, Zaher and Taher started devoting more time and attention to their own, determined not to suffer a similar fate.

Hafiz and I usually enjoyed teasing our friends about this, but tonight, our conversation was focused on more serious matters.

Omar informed us about the deteriorating political situation in Herat since the Russian invasion a month before, and Hafiz and I filled them in on what was happening in Kabul. When I told them about my experiences in *Sedarat* -- the torture and all the killing -- the brothers were shocked and saddened.

After discussing the matter, Zaher and Taher both decided that it would be best if they, too, left the country, and Omar encouraged them. "If I were younger, I'd want to go, too," he told us, "but I have my family to provide for and my job. I have to stay."

Hafiz and I stayed with Omar's family for two days, never leaving the house, while he made the necessary arrangements for our escape. Before the Russian invasion, crossing the border into Iran was no problem, but now it was very dangerous. Women and small children were still permitted to leave, but any man from his teens through middle age was certain to be detained, arrested or shot.

On our final evening in Herat, Omar gave us detailed instructions for our journey -- where to go, and who our contacts would be. Once this was done, the five of us sat in pensive silence, feeling reluctant to say goodnight, because in reality, we were really saying goodbye.

When, if ever, would we have the chance to be together again? Considering the uncertainty of our future, the only phrase that came to mind was, "*In Shalah* ... God willing .... we would someday meet again.

Chapter 21

THE FOUR OF of us left Herat in the pre-dawn darkness of a cold February morning. Our guide for the first stage of the journey was a bearded Afghan in his mid-thirties who owned a very old American Jeep. Avoiding the paved roads where there were Russian blockades every five miles, he headed west across the rough desert terrain.

The city of Herat lies some eighty miles from the border between Afghanistan and Iran, and while we had no blockades to contend with, our progress was frustratingly slow and not without its share of danger. Russian surveillance helicopters frequently flew over the area, and whenever our guide spotted one of these deadly birds of prey, he quickly brought the Jeep to a stop. The reason for this being, the Russians were less likely to become suspicious at the sight of a stationary vehicle than one speeding toward the border.

This stop-and-go driving was nerve-racking for everyone, and I soon lost count of all the stops. It was fully light and we had been on the road a few hours when the Jeep came to an unexpected, sputtering stop -- this time with no helicopters in sight.

After several unsuccessful attempts to start the engine, the guide finally got out and lifted up the hood. Hafiz, who knew a little something about cars, got out as well and offered his assistance. The guide had no idea what was wrong, but after checking a few things, Hafiz came back to tell us he was fairly sure the problem was with the carburator.

Identifying a problem and being able to solve it are two very different things. After working on the Jeep for over an hour in the cold and the wind, Hafiz finally gave up and said he needed a better place to work and the proper tools in order to make the repairs.

Fortunately for us, the Jeep had broken down near a small village some two hundred yards away. We all got out, and after locking the vehicle, started walking toward the village.

As we drew closer, we were met by a bunch of curious children. Hafiz and I let Zaher and Taher do most of the talking since Heratees have an accent which is very different from the people of Kabul. Zaher asked a small boy with close-cropped dark hair where we could find help, and the boy told us to follow him.

The village was typical of most Afghan settlements -- sparse trees, and a few muddy-brick houses with high walls surrounding them. The boy stopped beside a large door on one of the walls, and after asking us to please wait there, he went inside.

A tall man with broad shoulders, a black beard and a black turban came to the door moments later.

"Salam," he said politely and shook our hands. "What can I do to help you?"

Zaher explained our situation -- that we were on our way to the border and our Jeep had broken down just outside the village. The man listened, nodded, then gestured to the yard inside the walls. "Please come in."

The courtyard was very large with several fruit trees in the middle. In spring and summer, I'm sure it would be a pleasant place, but now the branches were bare and the wind was bitter. The L-shaped rooms of the house were located on the north and west sides of the yard. Through one of the windows, I saw someone watching our approach.

We were all feeling a little nervous as a tall, silver-bearded old man with a turban left the house and approached us. He was wearing traditional Afghan clothes and the long quilted coat called a *Chapan* . Through the thick lens of his glasses, I could see big brownish eyes surrounded by crows feet that added more charm to his kind face.

Sensing our nervousness, the old man offered a humble smile, then said with a soft, trembling voice, "*Salam,* my sons."

In my country, out of respect, people address an elderly man as 'uncle' or 'father.' The moment we heard him use the word 'sons,' we knew that we would be welcome in his house.

The old man turned slowly and asked us to follow him to the guest room. This was fairly small, no more than 6' x 7', with a ceiling made of exposed beams and rushes plastered with clay. The walls were painted white and decorated only by some pictures of the holy city of Mecca. In the middle of the room I saw a *sandaly* covered with a big comforter. A few mattresses had been placed on the earthen floor, and there were several large pillows leaning against wooden crates.

As we sat down, the old man seated himself at the head of the *sandaly* and told the black-bearded man to bring us tea.

After asking our names and where we came from, the old man looked at us and said, "You are leaving the country."

His words were a statement, rather than a question.

We hesitated a moment, then Zaher answered, "Yes, Father, we are."

The old man sat in silence, slowly shaking his head. He drew a deep breath, then said, "I did not want to see this moment in my life. All these young people ... the seed and fruit of our country ... leaving."

I was touched by the sadness in his face and his voice.

Minutes later, the black-bearded man returned with the tea and some cookies. When we had finished eating, the old man told us we had better see if there was someone in the village who could help us repair the Jeep. Then he invited us to come back and spend the night with him.

The people in the village were very poor, but what they had, they gladly shared with us. Thanks to their kindness, Hafiz was able to find the necessary tools and help he needed. A few hours later, the Jeep's engine was running smoothly once more.

Although we were eager to continue our journey, by now, the winter afternoon was waning. Hafiz felt it would be wise if we accepted the old man's invitation and spend the night here. "We might learn some helpful directions," he added, and we all agreed.

Our guide parked the Jeep in front of the old man's house and the same black-bearded man who had answered our knock before, ushered us inside and to the guest room.

We were warming ourselves around the *sandaly* when the old man entered the room and took his place at the head of the long, low table.

He broke the silence by saying simply, "So you got the car fixed."

Zaher answered, "Yes, sir."

The old man was silent for a long moment, moving his head back and forth as he ran his fingers through his silvery beard.

"When I was your age, I was in the army serving King Amanullah," he told us. "I felt so good and so proud serving him. What a king! During the holy month of Ramazan he would gather all the poor people of the town into a huge place and feed them. King Amanullah ate and prayed with them. Sometimes he disguised himself as one of the homeless to find out how the unfortunate people lived. He really cared about his people."

All of us were familiar with King Amanullah from studying the history of Afghanistan in school, but we hadn't heard this particular story. The way the old man talked made it even more fascinating and real than anything I had read in books.

Our host was still speaking with us when the black-turbaned man entered the room and said, "Dinner is ready, Grandpa."

As the food was set on our small table, the old man lifted a trembling hand to give us some advice. "Wherever you go, wherever you eat, don't be shy. Eat as much as you can. If it's a friend's house, he'll be happy. If it's an enemy's house, it will bother him. Either way you are a winner."

I smiled at his wisdom. These words put us completely at ease and we we were happy to follow his advice. After everyone had eaten his fill, the old man went on to give us additional counsel for our upcoming journey.

"You are going to another country with a different culture and different people," he said. "You shouldn't expect the same things you had here. You will meet some nice people, but also some who will try to take advantage of you. Understand yourselves before you get in the crowd." He paused a moment to put some tobacco in his Afghan pipe, then put the end of the long hose in his mouth.

Hafiz, who was sitting closest to the old man, took some matches from his pocket and lit the tobacco. Our host gestured his thanks by gently tapping Hafiz's hand.

The old man took five or six drags of tobacco, his eyes focused on the pipe, as he gathered his thoughts. "You know," he said, "things will be different in Iran than you are used to." He went on to repeat many of his earlier instructions to us, wisps of smoke curling from his mouth as he spoke. "Understand yourselves before you get in the crowd," he said again, in that trembling, wise voice.

Reading the acceptance of his advice in our eyes and open faces, the old man went on to share many other ideas and philosophies.

The details of that scene will always be vivid in my mind. The yellow-white glare and hiss of a single gas lantern ... the play of light and shadow on my friends' and my brother's faces ... the old man's wise, yet wavering voice ... and the soft curls of smoke coming from his mouth.

After a moment of thoughtful silence, he concluded, "You know, human emotions and feelings are like a river -- wild and powerful. When a river finds lower ground it runs savagely, careless of what it might harm in its path. This action will either take the river to the deserts where it dries without giving any service to nature, or it may run through the beautiful, proud mountains, creating green and exciting places on its journey to the ocean."

I was fascinated with his symbolic word painting of a river and life. Something inside me knew that from then on, whenever I heard the word river, the message of this night would start dancing with the music of my memories.

The old man got stiffly to his feet. "My dear sons, you have to get some rest. Tomorrow will be a big day for you. I will see you in the morning. *In Shalah*."

After he left the room, we lay down on the mattresses and pillows, with our feet tucked under the *sandaly* to keep warm. Pulling the soft quilts up around our chins, we settled down in the comforting darkness.

"That old man reminds me of a poem." My brother's soft voice spoke out of the darkness. "... *My heart is warm with the heat of love, but my head is silver because of pain and age. I feel like I am hiding a red ball of fire under my ashes.*"

He couldn't have described him better.

* * *

About three-thirty in the morning, the black-bearded man came into our room to wake us up. He showed us a manual pump where we could wash, and afterwards, we returned to the guest room to find our breakfast waiting, and the old man sitting at the head of the *sandaly* .

When we finished eating, I made the mistake of trying to offer our host a couple hundred *afghanis* for his generosity. I could see this made him feel very uncomfortable.

"Guests are friends of Allah," he told me. "I wouldn't want to take advantage of Him."

I was embarrassed for having offended him.

Sensing this, he added, "You are very young. You are entitled to make your mistakes. Just don't forget that Afghans are hospitable."

We thanked him, said our goodbyes, and drove away while the stars' pale light was still glowing in the winter sky.

After traveling for ten miles or so, our guide informed us that it was too dangerous for him to take us any further. He tore a ten *afghani* bill in two, and handed half to Hafiz.

"When you get to Quizilislam, ask for Nassir and give him the money. He'll take care of you." Then, pointing to the west, he said, "Keep going that way. Don't stop and go as fast as you can!"

Something in his voice set the blood pounding through our veins, and we headed off through the near-darkness of the snow-covered desert.

We had gone barely a half mile, when I realized Zaher was lagging far behind. I could hear his panting breaths somewhere behind me as he begged Taher to help him with his bags.

Unlike the rest of us, Taher had insisted on taking two large suitcases filled with his favorite suits, shoes, sweaters and other expensive clothes.

Taher grudgingly carried one of the heavy cases for another hundred yards or so, then told his brother he'd have to handle his own luggage.

It wasn't long after that before I heard Zaher's voice calling out from the darkness behind me, "Dear Ahmad! You know how much I love you. More than any of my brothers."

"Zaher," I said, "if you think you can 'sweet talk' me intohelping you with your bags, don't waste your energy."

Turning around, I could make out the outline of Zaher's dark figure staggering across the snow, a heavy suitcase in each hand.

"Give me one of the bags," I said, "but hurry."

By now, the darkness had diluted to a fuzzy gray, and Zaher's vanity was seriously impeding our progress. We struggled on this way for another hundred yards or so, until finally, I knew something had to be done about the situation.

I stopped where I was, opened my bag and took out my diplomas and a few cassett tapes. The tapes I stuffed in my pockets, and the diplomas, which had been wrapped in plastic for protection, I slipped inside my shirt. Then, after swinging the suitcase back and forth, I threw it as far as I could.

After watching me, Hafiz and Taher stopped and did the same.

From behind, we heard Zaher's puffing approach. "Oh, good! Now you can all help me!"

"Only in your dreams!" his brother answered.

Zaher caught up with us and gasped, "I'm going to hate you all for this!"

"Not when we're trying to save your life," I told him.

In that moment, Zaher finally understood the seriousness of our situation. That there was no going back. If we were caught, it meant imprisonment or death.

Setting the luggage down, he frantically sorted through his clothes, grabbing favorite things and putting them on, one on top of the other. "I would hate to see some Russian wearing these beautiful clothes," he muttered.

Under different circumstances, I would have laughed at the sight of him wearing so many layers, but by now, I was feeling too much urgency to be on our way.

As the winter dawn approached behind our backs, we tried to increase our pace, but the rough terrain and snowy ground and made it impossible to run.

Many times, the layers of ice under the snow gave way under our weight, and our shoes sank into icy water. In places where the snow wasn't as deep, we found ourselves traveling through mud. At times, it almost seemed to me as if the mud were alive and trying to stop us by snatching the shoes off our feet. Each time it did, precious seconds were lost going back to get them, then struggling to put them back on.

Soon after the sun rose, we heard the roar of Russian helicopters. For us, those throbbing metal wings were the sound of death. Hearing the sound, the four of us would frantically dive for some place to hide -- a rock, a bush, whatever we could find.

In spite of the danger, our fears and the cold, there was a strong sense of security among us. We were like four brothers, traveling side by side, taking the biggest step of our lives into the unknown.

Around two o'clock in the afternoon, we reached the crest of a small hill. From its vantage point we could see the muddy-brick houses of a small village some distance away. The sight filled us with excitement and renewed energy, as we ran down the hill. Until that moment, none of us was sure if we were going in the right direction or not.

As we neared the village of Quizilislam, we were met by four bearded men wearing *paculis* on their heads and carrying machine guns in their hands.

The men knew immediately by our appearance that we were victims of the invasion. One of them stepped forward and shook our hands.

"Welcome to the land of the free! The land of *mujahidin!*"

Hearing those beautiful words, we couldn't stop the tears from running down our cheeks.

A few weeks earlier, I could never in my wildest dreams have imagined such a scene, but to me, this little village was like paradise and the people were angels.

As we talked with the *mujahidin,* it was obvious they didn't have a college or even a high school education, but these men were highly educated in the love of their country, their people and in the love of freedom. Looking at the glowing circle of eyes that hadn't had a good night's rest in weeks, and dry lips that hadn't touched a decent meal in God knows how long, I could feel their love and their pain.

Walking into the village that winter afternoon, accompanied by these ragged, but proud guardians of freedom, the words of a song impressed themselves upon my mind: "If the wound in my chest would let me take my hand off my heart, I would write the word of freedom all over my country with my blood .... "

One of the *mujahidin* remained with us when we reached the village walls, while the rest went their way.

"We receive lots of refugees here," he told us. "We can't provide food and shelter for all of them. As you know, we don't have anyone except Allah to help us. But I'm sure He knows we are doing our best. On the other side of the village there is an old castle by the river. You can go out there and wait."

"Do you know a man by the name of Nassir?" Hafiz asked.

"Everybody around here knows Nassir, but he won't be back until tomorrow. I'll let him know that you're looking for him when I see him." Saying this, the man bid us goodbye and went on his way.

In the village, we found a small bakery and stopped to buy some bread. Next to the bakery was a grocery store. The only food it had to offer was a little dried fruit, which we were grateful to buy.

We divided the warm bread and dried fruit among us as we walked along. The winter afternoon was waning and we had come a long way since our last meal at the home of the old man. I don't know if it was our hunger, the food, or my companions on this journey -- perhaps it was all three -- but that was one of the most memorable meals of my life.

Just past the village, we came to the ruins of an ancient castle. The *caravanserie* had four high walls, but no doors or rooms. A few brick walls inside the *caravanserie's* huge courtyard were the only remnants of a building that no longer existed.

As we entered, we saw refugees sitting around campfires that had been built in different corners of the yard. From behind one of the center walls, we heard the sound of small children crying and knew that must be the place designated for women, so they could have some privacy to feed their babies.

The four of us joined a group of people sitting around one of the fires and tried to make ourselves comfortable for the night. There were easily two hundred or more people huddled within the ruins of the old *caravanserie*. As night fell, everyone was quiet except for the fascinated laughter of a dozen or so children who were making circles in the air with long, smoking sticks.

I watched the colorful shapes and circles dancing in the night air, finding myself as fascinated as the children with these rustic toys. The burning sticks looked like little rainbows glowing in the dark.

Around the fire, our circle was growing larger. In order to make room for the newcomers who wanted to join us, we all squeezed closer together. So close, that when I looked at my brother's face, I could see a little reflection of the fire in Hafiz' eyes.

As the night grew riper, the crackling cries of the fire echoed against the proud, tall walls of the old castle. The sound was like the music of fireworks coming from far away to whisper into our ears, the prelude of a new and uncertain spring in this, the coldest season of our lives.

chapter 22

THE WINTER MORNING was brisk and the skies clear as I walked to the river with my brother, Zaher and Taher to wash. Any traces of sleep or weariness were quickly wiped away by the shock of icy water on our skin.

Someone before us had left an old teapot behind, which we gratefully adopted to heat water for some tea. All we could find were two old cups, so everyone around the fire took turns drinking the tea.

No one in the *caravanserie* knew when we would be allowed to cross the river. For this we had to trust the information and wisdom of the *mujahidin* in the village. Although the rebels frequently sneaked back and forth across the border, it wasn't safe for us to cross the Hari Rode during the day because of the Russian patrols and surveillance helicopters. The rest of the people in the old castle were just like us ... waiting.

Around three in the afternoon we met our contact, Nassir. He took the *afghani* bill that had been given to us by our first guide, then ripped an Iranian bill in half, and instructed us to give it to our Iranian contact on the other side. Pointing to a large clump of willows across the river, Nassir showed us where we should wait for our guide.

"Tonight is a good night to cross the river," he said, "but first, we'll need you to help us make the *jalas.*"

We were excited by this news and eager to help. The four of us hurried down to the river bank where many people were already hard at work making the rafts which would carry us across the Hari Rode. Constructed of inflated animal skins tied to wooden boards or logs, *jalas* are unique to Afghanistan, and have been used for many centuries to cross its rushing rivers.

We had only a few hours until dark, and there were hundreds of people hoping to cross the Hari Rode -- men, women, children and small babies. To get the work down faster and more efficiently, we formed an assembly line of sorts. Everyone did his part, whether it was gathering and assembling the wood, or inflating the animal skins. Most of these were the insides of cattle or sheep, and blowing up these giant, tough-skinned balloons soon had us puffing and out of breath.

After making a dozen or more *jalas* , there was nothing to do now but wait. Nassir had said we wouldn't be leaving until it was fully dark, and even then, we had to wait for a signal from the other side.

The word came just before midnight. The rebels moved quietly among us, instructing everyone not to run, or make any noise. I'm sure this must have been very difficult for the mothers with young children, but thankfully, most of the little ones were asleep by this time. Silently, the young men helped the women, children and older men onto the *jalas*. Then, holding onto the sides of the raft, we waded into the cold river and pushed the *jalas* across the rushing current. A full moon shining overhead helped guide us through the watery path to freedom.

The swiftly flowing current, the strong element of danger and the silent faces of the people huddled on the rafts made an indelible impression on my mind. Because of the large number of people wanting to cross, the men had to make several trips, ferrying the rafts back and forth across the river. Even with our youth and strength, the icy water soon took its toll.

After five or six bone-chilling trips, I stood on the Iranian side of the Hari Rode, waiting for Taher and Zaher to join Hafiz and me. My wet, dripping clothes felt much colder and heavier than they had a few minutes earlier. Pressing my teeth together in order to keep them from chattering, I stared across the river to my homeland.

I was frightened -- frightened of the unknown future, for my country, my family and friends, and for the people of Afghanistan. But in my heart, I had the feeling of a burning flame, the flame of freedom and dignity, that had been lost at the hands of the Russians and the brutal agents of KhAD.

As my eyes focused on the moon's shimmering reflection on the surface of the river, its silvery round face seemed to be reflecting the wise, friendly face of the old man I had met two days earlier. In my mind, I could hear his words of counsel, especially his beautiful words comparing life to a river.

Suddenly, it was not only the face of the old man that I was seeing on the surface of the river, but the faces of my family, my friends, my former life and my dearest country that I was leaving behind for the unknown future.

Even though I was shivering and cold, I lingered on the river bank a few more moments, wanting to keep with me forever that last beautiful image of my country.

Taher and Zaher joined Hafiz and me a few seconds later, and although no one said a word, we could understand each other's thoughts. We were all thinking the same thing. We had just left our country ....

* * *

The four of us had waited in the clump of trees for close to an hour before we heard someone walking toward us through the darkness.

A young Iranian man emerged from the dark trees and asked softly, "Who told you to wait here?"

"Nassir," Taher answered, just as softly.

The man nodded his satisfaction then said, "Follow me."

We had traveled several hundred yards through brushy, wooded terrain when a flashlight's strong beam stopped us in our tracks. Caught in the circle of light, we stood motionless.

Out of the darkness beyond the light came a sharp command. "Put your hands up and don't make a move."

Two soldiers, one with a rifle, and the other carrying the flashlight approached. "Who are you?" asked the man with the rifle.

"We are refugees from Afghanistan," Zaher answered.

"You're not smugglers or anything?" he said, as the soldier with the flashlight searched us one by one.

"No. Only refugees."

Something in the tone of their voices eased our fears. After searching us, the soldier joined his companion and they stood a few yards off, whispering together,

Then one of them said, "Just go -- get out of here, fast!"

We didn't need further encouragement to follow his advice.

Walking swiftly ahead, our guide led the way through the moonlit night, instructing us to pick up any broken branches or wood we might find along the way. "You're going to need them for a fire later," he explained shortly.

Of that we had no doubt. With four or five inches of snow on the ground, and icy, wet clothes clinging to our bodies, we were already freezing. The four of us stumbled along behind the guide for several miles, pausing only to pick up a little brush or kindling.

Finally, the Iranian stopped and pointed to a small gleam of light piercing the darkness. "There's a farmer's house up ahead. They usually help refugees. Give me the bill and good luck to you."

Taher handed him the money and we walked on toward the light. When we reached the small farm house, Zaher knocked on the door, while the rest of us waited at the gate. An old lady answered his knock, and he quickly explained that we were refugees from Afghanistan and needed shelter for the night.

The woman was not happy about being roused from her bed, but for a goodly sum of money, she gave us some bread and water and allowed us to spend the night in the stable.

"There's a town a few miles to the west where you can find transportation and food," she said, adding, "but you'll have to get there early to catch the truck."

We paid her for the food, then headed wearily for the stable and set about building a fire. Standing in front of its crackling warmth, we chewed the hard bread and gulped the water.

Everyone was exhausted from the night's work and crossing the river many times. In spite of the cold, we barely finished eating before falling asleep near the fire's cozy warmth.

We woke at first light to discover it had snowed during the night. The stable had no doors or covering for the windows to keep out the weather, so our little shelter was liberally powdered with white. In order to keep from freezing, we knew we had to keep moving.

After a cold two or three mile walk, we saw the welcome sight of some farmers' houses just ahead. Nearby, two men were loading sheep from a wooden corral into a large truck.

Zaher approached one of the men, and asked if he would be willing to give us a ride to Mashad.

The farmer smiled. "If you help me load the sheep, you've got yourself a deal, but it's going to be a rough ride."

We were so eager to give our feet a rest, we didn't realize how right he was about that ride. After most of the sheep were loaded, the four of us climbed into the back and lay down, one on each side of the truck. By the time the rest of the animals joined us, the place was like a crowded zoo, where we were the floor and the sheep did whatever they wanted.

Things got even rougher once we were on our way. The dirt road we were traveling had lots of bumps and pot holes which jostled the sheep on all sides.

After fifteen minutes or so, I heard Zaher screaming, "I can't take it any more! I'm going to die! I'd rather be tortured by Communists. At least that would be a decent death."

"Shut up, Zaher," I said. "If you were under the Communist torture, what the sheep are doing to you, you'd be doing in your pants."

We drove for perhaps another hour, then we heard Zaher complaining again. "Oh God, I've got something in my mouth ...."

"Good! Don't you get it? Even the sheep are trying to keep you quiet."

"You guys are sick," he answered. "How can you handle the smell? Why do these animals smell so bad anyway, and why do we eat them?"

We knew if we kept answering him, he'd never stop talking, so we stayed quiet and tried to keep our faces covered.

After a smelly hour's journey, the truck stopped at a check-point and this time, no one had to ask Zaher to stay silent. We were all holding our breath.

I heard someone ask the driver, "What do you have in the back?" Then his answer, "Just some sheep."

A tense moment passed, then we heard a tapping noise on the side of the truck and the man's voice told the driver to move on.

A short while later, the truck stopped again. But this time, we heard the driver's friendly voice telling us, "This is Mashad. You can get out now."

Hafiz was closest to the door, and the first to leave our smelly zoo. As the rest of us shoved our way past the sheep, we could hear the driver laughing hysterically and wondered what was going on. The minute we climbed out of the truck and saw each other's faces and clothes, we knew why he was laughing so hard. Our hair, our faces, our clothes and our shoes were all covered with yellow and green spots and other signs of a very rough trip with animals. Soon, we were all laughing.

We thanked the driver and offered him some money, which he refused. "Over there is the famous mosque, Amam Raza," he told us. "You can go there to wash yourselves. No one will bother you."

As we walked toward the mosque, all the people on the street were staring at us. God only knows what they were thinking, but it didn't really matter. Still, every time I looked at Zaher and his once-beautiful clothes liberally covered with sheep dung, I couldn't wipe the smile off my face.

Inside the mosque we found a beautiful large courtyard where there was water to wash ourselves and our clothes. The day was still a bit cold, but at least the sun was shining, and for the moment, we knew we were safe.

It must have taken a good three to four hours for us to get clean, shave and look like human beings again. While we waited for our clothes to dry, I walked around the courtyard looking at the colorful walls of mosaic tile, and reading the religious poems and verses from the Holy Koran which were inscribed upon them.

Emotion welled up inside me, and soon, tears were running down my face. I found a secluded spot in one of the corners of the mosque and offered a prayer, thanking God for His help in getting us safely out of the country. I asked Him from the sincerest part of my heart to help my family and my country through the difficult times ahead.

In spite of the tears and the sadness, I got up from my knees feeling better than I had in a long time, and never doubting that God would answer my prayer and give me the strength to deal with whatever the future might bring.

The others were waiting for me at the mosque entrance. Looking into their faces, I knew we were experiencing similar emotions. Without a word, we put our arms around each other's shoulders and left the mosque.

Naturally, it was Zaher who introduced a practical element into the day. "Aren't you guys starving?" he asked. "Let's go eat!"

We laughingly agreed and headed toward a restaurant with a warm feeling of friendship and a sense of dignity inside our hearts. We were becoming part of "the crowd" as the old man had said. And we each knew this trip would someday be one of the most wonderful memories of our lives.

Chapter 23

UNLIKE OUR JOURNEY from Mashad to Tehran, we arrived in Iran's largest city in the comfort of a Mercedes Benz bus.

It was a Friday morning and the streets were jammed with traffic. We had no difficulties finding a taxi, but the drive through the huge city to the home where my sister Rahella and her husband Anwar were living, seemed to take forever.

"First it's sheep, now it's cars," Zaher grumbled as the taxi crawled along through one traffic jam after another.

When we reached Anwar's and Rahella's home, the front door was ajar. We entered without knocking and walked across the small courtyard which led to the house itself.

Rahella, Anwar and a few of his relatives were sitting crosslegged on the floor, eating lunch around a small table cloth as we entered the room. My sister glanced up and when she saw Hafiz and me, her eyes opened wide. Color rushed into her face, then tears began to flow down her beautiful red cheeks.

"My dear God, you're alive and you're here," she said in a trembling voice.

She got to her feet and we went into each other's arms, holding each other and crying freely. Soon, we were all hugging each other and crying.

Rahella finally gathered enough control to invite us to sit down and have lunch with them. I was touched as I watched my beautiful sister trying to control her excitement by being the best hostess she could be. She refused to let any of us do anything for ourselves.

Afterwards, while we were drinking tea, Rahella sat next to me, holding my hand, and asking questions about our family and everyone in Afghanistan. When she asked about my ordeal in *Sedarat*, I kept my answers brief and tried to give her the impression that what I had been through wasn't a big deal. Besides the fact she was pregnant with her first child, I didn't want to upset her and spoil her happiness in seeing us again.

We allowed ourselves a few days to rest and enjoy our family, then Hafiz and I started looking for work. I had been given the address of a young Iranian by the name of Mahmood, whose father used to work at the Iranian Embassy in Kabul. Mahmoood had been one of my classmates at the University. I remembered him as a short, chubby man with curly hair. During our first few days at college, it seemed like he wore a different suit every day. He always looked like a prince. Most of the other students came from poor families and bought their clothes from the American second-hand bazaar. By the following week, Mahmood began to realize why the students felt so uncomfortable around him. One day he walked into class wearing clothes just like us, and little by little we became friends.

Mahmood was very happy to see me, when I visited him at his home in Tehran, and graciously offered me a room. I thanked him but declined, explaining that I wanted to stay with my family. The next morning Mahmood arrived at Anwar's house with a stack of different newspapers listing various jobs that were available. Zaher was the only one who found a job easily because he was a trained pharmacist.

After hunting for two weeks, the only position Hafiz and I could get was at a chicken farm, cleaning up after the chickens. I soon learned that when thousands of these little creatures get together they can make a very big mess.

At the end of three weeks, I was so tired of chickens that I never wanted to see or eat one again. On my days off I looked for another job, but with no success. Finally, Taher and I decided to open our own business. We bought several different items, such as hats, cassettes, socks, pencils, etc., from Bandirabass, and joined the thousands of people who sold their wares on the famous street of Musadiq.

For three days, neither one of us sold a single item. On the fourth day I was attempting to sell a hat to a young student named Hussein. He immediately noticed my accent and asked where I was from.

When he learned we were from Afghanistan, Hussein expressed a lot of interest in the political situation and asked many questions about the country. Then he grinned at me and said, "Watch closely. I'm going to show you how to sell things here."

The next thing I knew, Hussein was stopping people who were passing by, and bragging about the quality and cheap prices of my merchandise. He was so good that in a matter of an hour or two he sold over half of what I had. From then on, Hussein came by every day after his college classes to help us sell. With his help, our business rapidly improved, and soon, I began to learn a few of his tricks.

One day when Hussein came to see us, he brought a large amount of money with him. "This is my life savings and my college tuition and expenses," he told me. "I know I can manage somehow, and I want to use this money to help the refugees."

I was touched by my new friend's intentions, but wondered how he was going to do this. Later that afternoon, Hussein asked me to I accompany him to a large apartment complex where many Afghan refugees had been fortunate enough to obtain housing. The apartments were small, most of them only two rooms, and not in very good condition. But at least the people had a roof over their heads and conditions there were far better than in refugee camps outside the city.

To my amazement, Hussein walked through the apartment building, giving away all his college money and savings to the refugees. And this he did with a big smile on his face.

At one point, I had to ask why he was doing this.

"I can imagine how it must feel -- these poor people living in such horrible conditions without any hope or help," he said. "I can hear them calling the name of God, asking for help. I love God, and whenever I think I hear someone calling His name, I want to do everything that is in my power to answer."

I will never forget Hussein or his generosity. In fact, the kindness of this one person made it easy for me to forget all the others who resented the presence of Afghan refugees in Iran.

* * *

A month or so after our arrival in Iran, my wife and son along with my cousin Faquir were able to join us. Fortunately, it wasn't as difficult in those days for women and children to leave Afghanistan and they encountered no danger in coming to us.

With ten people living in a small two-room house, conditions were very crowded. The women and children slept in the bedroom, while the rest of us, slept in the living room or outside in the yard. During the day, the men went to work and at night we would return with a bag of food or fruit to share with everyone else. Zaher always made sure that we took our vitamins because he was able to get free samples from the pharmacy. Especially Rahella, since she was pregnant.

As weeks passed, I felt more and more confident in my small selling business. I wasn't making a lot of money, just enough for us to survive, but there was a welcome sense of security living in Iran, away from KhAD and the Communists. The culture wasn't too different from our own, and soon, I began making new friends.

One night when I returned home from work, and immediately noticed that my family seemed very worried and tense. When I asked what had happened, my wife explained that it had just announced on the radio that "for environmental and municipal reasons," all the street sellers would have two days to pack up their merchandise and get off the streets. Otherwise, the police would do it for them."

This news was like a hammer striking a blow to my nervous system. The first question that came to my mind was, "How am I going to feed my family? In a single moment, all the feelings of security were gone, but I didn't want the others to know how concerned I was.

"Don't worry," I told them with a confidence I didn't really feel. "I'll find another job."

The situation grew even worse when fighting broke out between Iran and Iraq. Listening to the news from day to day, I decided to visit the French Embassy in Tehran, to see if I could obtain a refugee visa for France. After filling out numerous forms and waiting for days, I was able to arrange a meeting with the man in charge. He informed me that unless I had an important position in the Afghan government, or could prove that my life was in danger here in Iran, he wouldn't be able to help me.

This was very disappointing news, because I couldn't prove either one.

As we searched for another solution, my wife mentioned that she had four brothers who were citizens of the United States. Perhaps they could help us.

A few weeks later we received a letter from Zar's brother Abdul. He wrote that he had made several inquiries on our behalf, but the political situation between the U.S. and Iran was so strained as a result of the current hostage situation, that nothing could be done for us. Abdul suggested that we consider going to Pakistan instead.

The letter wasn't very encouraging, but it was our only hope. After giving the matter a lot of consideration, Hafiz and the others decided they would stay on in Iran.

A few days later, my wife and son, along with Rahella and Anwar, took a bus to Zahedan near the Iran/Pakistani border. Along with our few possessions, our entire fortune amounted to roughly $120. Besides the lack of money, there was another cause for worry. None of us had visas or passports to enter Pakistan. This added additional weight to my concerns because an acquaintance in Iran had told me if I got caught, I'd be sent directly to the border and handed over to the Communist authorities.

If I had been alone and single, I'm not sure I would have had the courage to take such a big step. But I had Jossef, and if there were only the smallest chance of providing him with the opportunity to grow up in a peaceful country, I would gladly have taken any risk.

After reaching Zahedon, we were only hours away from that hell called the border. By afternoon, I was unable to hide my growing nervousness. Telling the others I needed some fresh air, I left our hotel room and started walking down the main road.

In the median strip between the two-way street, a few trees and some grass had been planted. Here, I saw four Afghans playing cards. Gathering my courage, I approached them and asked if it was possible for me to go in to Pakistan without a passport.

Sensing my fear, one of the men looked up at me and said, "What kind of an Afghan are you, if you can't even go to Pakistan?"

Even though I was embarrassed by the remark, his words were like a mountain of encouragement. I walked away with a renewed sense of determination and returned to my family. With a convincing tone and lots of bragging, I told them not to worry, that going to Pakistan would be a 'glass of water.'

The next morning we caught a bus that took us to the border between Iran and Pakistan. When we arrived at the crossing, the bus stopped and a group of soldiers approached us.

They ordered all the passengers to get off the bus and leave their luggage and personal belongings behind. Nervously, we did as they asked, then watched while some of the soldiers entered the bus and started searching through the passengers' bags and possessions. A few more climbed on top of the bus and shuffled through the suitcases that had been stowed there. When they finished, we were told to go back inside and get out our passports and visas.

The only papers my family and I had to show them were some personal identification and my diplomas from school.

The soldiers began checking passengers from both ends of the bus. When they reached us, I explained that we were refugees from Afghanistan.

The soldier questioning me said, "Wait here," then got off the bus to find his superior officer. In the few moments it took for the officer to arrive, we were all frozen with fear.

I don't think that officer had any idea that he held the destiny of five people in his hands, or that he could be the one to send me back to the horrors of a living hell called *Sedarat*.

Approaching us, he asked in a low, kind voice, "Are you from Afghanistan?"

"Yes," I said. "We're going to Peshawar to escape from Communism."

As the officer stared at each one of us, I felt the tension growing with every second that passed. Little Jossef was the only one who didn't seem at all worried about the situation. He kept smiling at the officer, who touched his round cheek with one finger and said, "Cute little *Patan*."

Then he turned to the soldier standing next to him and said, "Let them go."

As the bus continued on its way past the border, I wondered what it was that made him decide to let us go. Maybe it was the will of God. Or maybe he was just a good man and understood our struggle. Perhaps the government of Pakistan had something to do with it. Maybe all those reasons were hidden behind the innocent smile of my son-- the little *Patan*.

Upon our arrival in Quita we went directly to the train station and bought a ticket for Lahor. Two exhausting days of travel followed. When we arrived in Peshawar, our limited funds made it necessary to stay in the cheapest lodging we could find. One hundred *afghanis* converted into 10 *rupees*, and after considerable searching, we were able to find a hotel that cost us roughly $1 per night. The place was hot as hell, with no services and barely enough water for drinking. But we were safe and together.

As soon as I had my family settled, I went downstairs and made two phone calls -- the first to Zarguna's brothers in the United States, giving them our address and letting know we had arrived safely; the other to Tehran. When I talked with my brother Hafiz, he had some surprising news. My entire family -- father, mother, sisters and my youngest brother, had escaped from Afghanistan and were all in Tehran.

When Rahella heard this, she said she couldn't stay in Peshawar another day. She and Anwar left immediately to return to Tehran. They wanted me and my family to go with them, but I explained that there wasn't any future for me in Iran. I had to try something else.

The greatest difficulty during our stay in Pakistan was our financial situation. I bought the cheapest food that I could find, and often, I skipped lunch or dinner. The days and nights got longer and harder. Zarghuna and Jossef and I were just existing. Nothing more.

Most of our time was spent looking out the small window in our room which was on the third floor of the hotel. Below us, the streets were crowded with traffic and people and the busy movement of life, while in our room, everything seemed as if it were frozen in time. Even my son had lost his enthusiasm for running around like other children his age. Our only means of entertainment was to look out that small square window, hoping to someday see a familiar face and waiting for a miracle to happen.

At night, memories of *Sedarat* still haunted my dreams, but I knew better than to share any of this with my wife.

Two weeks later, the miracle happened. Zarghuna was sitting by the window with Jossef when I heard her scream, "I can't believe it! It's my brother Abdul!"

The next moment she was running down the stairs like a little girl to meet him. Zarghuna and Abdul hadn't seen each other for nearly twenty years and their reunion was emotional one for us all. That night, the three of us were so busy talking and catching up on each other's lives, we didn't sleep at all.

Abdul told us that the United States government allowed a certain number of Afghan refugees to enter the country, but the process was a lengthy one. He felt the best thing for us to do was get a tourist visa, then apply for political asylum.

Abdul accompanied me to the American Consulate in Peshawar. where we were ushered into the office of a tall, well-dressed American. The man shook our hands and politely invited us to sit down. I was so excited, even if I had known how to speak English, I wouldn't have known what to say. This was my very first handshake from an American.

Abdul explained our situation to the official and from time to time, he asked me questions, then translated my answers for the official. When the American asked where I had gotten my passport, I answered without hesitation, that the *mujahidin* had given it to me. This might not be according to regulation, but there was no way the Communist government would have allowed me to leave the country, let alone go to the United States.

After talking with us for a half hour or so, the official took our passports, stamped them and handed them back to my brother-in-law. I waited until we were outside, before asking him what had happened.

Abdul gave me a big smile. "He gave you a three month tourist visa and said you can apply for political asylum in the United States. He thinks you have an excellent chance of getting permanent residency."

I could hardly wait to share the good news with my wife. Over and over, I showed her the stamped passport and said, "Do you know what this stamp is? It is the stamp of freedom! The stamp of a big change in our lives It means that all our misery and dark days are over!"

The day of our departure finally arrived and during the first leg of the journey, we took a plane to Germany. When I was in college, we used to call Europe and other western nations the 'highland countries."

I looked out the plane window at the quilted landscape far below. "Can you believe it? We are in the highland countries now!"

My wife smiled and shook her head. "You are acting just like a little boy!"

"Of course I'm acting like a little boy," I responded. "This morning we were in Asia. Now we are in Europe! By tomorrow morning, we'll be in America. In a matter of twenty-four hours we will have been in three different continents. You can't imagine how far I've wanted to run away from KhAD and the KGB agents. Now it's really happening!" I breathed a grateful sigh and told her, "You can always tell a good year by its spring, and the coming spring looks very good!"

Chapter 24

"'The electricity from the sky destroyed my nest, but it also taught me to build my next house stronger and safer. Now, I don't know if I should think of the sky as an enemy for the destruction, or as a teacher for the lesson.'"

Indian poem

IT WAS AUTUMN, not spring, when the travel-weary Sharifi family ended their journey in Salt Lake City, Utah. Leaving the airport, Ahmad was amazed that Utah should feel so familiar. The rugged, protective mountains of the Wasatch Front were not unlike those surrounding Kabul. Even the climate was similar. Dry and sunny, with clear blue skies.

In spite of the language barrier and obvious differences in culture, Ahmad enjoyed the warm friendliness of the people, and something even more wonderful. For the first time in over a year, he felt completely safe.

Two of Zarghuna's brothers, Abdul and Noor, both made their homes in Utah, which made the adjustment even easier. Thanks to Abdul, the Sharifis were able to settle in a small rental house in an area of older homes. Ahmad was also given the use of an old truck which had belonged to Zarghuna's oldest brother Golamad, who had passed away only a few months before of a heart attack.

"No one can survive in America without a car," Abdul told Ahmad bluntly.

Ahmad didn't argue the point, but having a car and knowing how to drive one were far different things -- especially when the vehicle involved happened to be an old truck with a manual transmission.

Across the street from their rental house was a large, vacant field, and every day for the first ten days after their arrival, Ahmad would go there to practice his driving. Once in a while, Abdul dropped by to give him a few pointers, but most of the time, Ahmad was on his own. Hour after hour, he drove doggedly around the field, grinding gears and jerking along as he endeavored to master this new challenge. After a few days, he felt confident enough to set up an obstacle course of sorts, with crude markers made of rocks and wood. Often he spent five or six hours every day, depending upon the supply of gasoline, just driving around and around that empty field.

On September 25, exactly ten days after their arrival in Utah, Abdul took Ahmad to the Driver's License Division and explained to the employees that his brother-in-law had just arrived from Afghanistan and wanted to get his driver's license. All those hours in the field paid off, because Ahmad passed both the written and the driving test on his first try.

Afterwards, they drove downtown to celebrate, and Abdul explained the layout of the streets and how to find various addresses. Ahmad was impressed with Salt Lake's wide streets, the cleanliness, and how simply the city was laid out. As far as he was concerned, Salt Lake was the greatest city in the world.

With a six-month visa and a new driver's license in his wallet, Ahmad now had two more challenges to face. Learning the English language and getting a job to support his family. Abdul had given them a little money to get started, but Ahmad wanted to earn his own way as soon as possible. During the day, he attended English classes, and in the evening, he worked a part-time job.

Zarghuna's brother Noor had a small import business and suggested that Ahmad try selling Persian rugs and tapestries door to door. Ahmad didn't see how this would work when he couldn't even speak the language, but Noor insisted that didn't matter and wrote down a script for him to memorize. Ahmad had his doubts about the success of the venture, especially the prospect of arriving on a stranger's doorstep to deliver a memorized sales approach in strange-sounding English spoken with a French/Afghan accent. But he needed work, and since Noor had gone to the trouble of offering his help, the least he could do was give it a try.

Some people were very kind, and Ahmad even managed to sell a few rugs, but after two months of having doors slammed in his face, he knew he had to find regular employment.

Bright and early one morning, Ahmad drove the pick-up truck to the Job Service office, determined to find work. His English skills were still extremely limited, and after struggling through pages of various jobs that were available, he decided to apply for the highest paying one -- a position as machinist, which started at $4.25 an hour. That same day he experienced his first job interview with a man by the name of Michael Long.

After going over his application, Mr. Long asked Ahmad a few questions, most of which he didn't understand. Finally, he said, "How many languages do you speak, Mr. Sharifi?"

"Five."

Michael Long smiled at the young dark-eyed Afghan sitting in front of him and said, "You're hired."

Ahmad stared at the man with a puzzled expression. "What does that mean?"

His new boss grinned even wider. "It means, come to work Monday."

Understanding dawned. "This is wonderful!" Ahmad told his new employer. "I not only have a job -- I know two new words for my vocabulary. You're hired!"

Months went by, filled with exciting new experiences and the challenge of mastering a new job, along with learning the language. Yet, no matter how busy he kept during the day, Ahmad's nights were still haunted by memories and nightmares of *Sedarat*. Just when he thought he had succeeded in pushing the past away, there would come a night when he woke up in a cold sweat, heart pounding, the screams of torture echoing in his ears. Sometimes, the sound of his own screams would wake both him and Zarghuna.

"It's all right," she would tell him. "Go back to sleep."

But it wasn't all right. And as time went on, Ahmad's greatest source of frustration was the steady deterioration of his marriage. He had known Zarghuna for several years before their arranged marriage had taken place. Her mother and Alima were first cousins and the two families were very close.

Although Ahmad was the first to admit that Zar was a fine person, he couldn't deny they were incompatible in several areas. From the beginning, they had had trouble communicating. And now, Ahmad could see the wall that had been built between them after his release from *Sedarat* growing larger and higher.

Very often, he found himself dreading the thought of returning home after work, which in turn, left him feel guilty and even more depressed.

Ahmad and Zarghuna had been living in Utah nearly four years when it became apparent she was pregnant with their second child. Both were excited at the prospect of having another baby, and during the months of pregnancy, their relationship was less strained than it had been for a long time.

About a month before the baby was due, Ahmad received an unexpected phone call from a friend of his brother Zoor. Ahmad was overjoyed to hear from a fellow

Afghan until the man said quietly, "May God forgive all his sins."

The expression was a common Afghan way of offering consolation after someone has died, to make death's message less painful for those who receive it.

"Whose sins?" Ahmad asked nervously.

"I'm sorry." There was a pause on the other end of the line. "Didn't you know your father has taken the last trip of his life?"

Ahmad couldn't speak. He hung up the phone, feeling too shocked for words -- even to cry. Inside him, there was a strong ache of disappointment that life had not given them the chance to be together one last time.

For weeks afterward, his father was constantly in Ahmad's thoughts. He found myself listening to the kind of music his father loved, and cooking his favorite dishes. Advice Latif had him given years before suddenly became more meaningful as loss bestowed Ahmad with painful appreciation for his father's wisdom.

As a young boy, Ahmad had been fascinated with the way his father talked and wished that he could express himself as well. Father and son had their first serious talk together on the evening of Ahmad's engagement party. Before the guests arrived, Latif had taken his son aside to share a few words of counsel.

He began the discussion by quoting an old Afghan saying: "If you don't have the heart of a lion, don't take the trip of love." Then he went on to tell Ahmad, "Marriage is one of the most serious and sacred commitments you will ever make. Just like life itself, it has its pain and its joy.

Pain is like salt, and joy is like sugar in our life. You cannot totally appreciate one without having tasted the other.

"Don't think this decision to marry is going to affect only you," he said. "We will all be affected by it, because a family is like a chain in the human body -- the weaknesses of one link affect the strength of the entire chain. If one part of the human body is in pain, the whole body suffers.

Latif smiled at his son. "There can't be a happier day for a father than to see his children pass on the torch of life from one generation to the next. Life is so short and uncertain. We humans are like a tear drop hanging on the eyelash, and tomorrow, I might not be here to tell you what I am trying to say today." He paused, then said, "Sharing your life with someone new is not easy. I'm sure she is going to make lots of mistakes, just as you will. Don't hate her for the mistakes that she makes, because hate is like a cancer tumor. It grows day by day and the one who suffers the most is the one who has it in his heart. Remember, Ahmad. The best revenge is forgiveness and the best weapon is humility. Always keep your heart open for love and your mind open for knowledge."

Latif went on talking, but Ahmad was getting tired and a little bored, like any young man who thinks he already knows everything and doesn't need any advice. Finally, he asked Ahmad if he was okay.

"I'm okay," Ahmad answered, "But I'm very confused now."

"Then I did my job right," his father answered. "Because confusion is the window to the garden of certainty."

This advice given so long ago, took on new meaning as Ahmad considered the present difficulties in his marriage. He had always hated arguing and conflicts of any kind. He needed to be more patient with Zar, especially now with a baby coming.

On July 4, 1984, Zarghuna gave birth to a healthy dark-eyed little boy. When Ahmad saw his new son for the first time, he was amazed and thrilled to discover the baby had so many features of his father.

"What would you think of giving him my father's name?" he asked Zarghuna tentatively.

"Latif?" she said. "I always liked that name."

The days and nights following Latif's birth were filled with the joy of a beautiful new life inside the Sharifi's small one-bedroom apartment. Where Ahmad had wanted to stay at work as long as possible, now he couldn't wait to go home and see the sparkle in Latif's dark eyes. The baby's resemblance to his father brought Ahmad much comfort. In many ways, he almost felt as if his father were alive again through this precious little son.

Latif was approaching his second birthday when a freak accident at work totally changed the comfortable pattern of Ahmad's life. One of his co-workers accidentally dropped a heavy steel plate on his right foot, crushing the bones and damaging many nerves and tissues.

After a lengthy hospital stay, Ahmad was required to stay in bed with his leg elevated for several months. The doctor prescribed some strong medication to help him deal with the pain, but the pills made him feel nauseated and drowsy. Knowing he would have to take the pain-killers over a long period of time, Ahmad was concerned about the potential risk of becoming addicted to the medication. Rather than do so, he stopped taking the pills. Non-prescription medication was totally useless, so he resigned himself to living with the pain.

For Ahmad, the call of pain was like the howling of wolves. During those long months of recovery, the throbbing heat of physical pain slowly melted the ice under which he had buried all the nightmares and horrible memories of his past.

He tried various methods of escape, but nothing worked. He couldn't read because the pain was so great, he couldn't grasp anything. After a while, he didn't enjoy watching television. Bored and frustrated, depression set in.

Ahmad started hating his life, then himself. Along with the physical pain, he was tortured by feelings of guilt. He felt guilty that he hadn't fought for his country like the *mujahidin* and countless other Afghans who had lost their lives ... guilty that he hadn't been present when his father died ... guilty for not loving his wife the way he was supposed to ... and guilty for putting some of the best years of his life into getting an education, then not being able to use what he had learned.

As the weeks passed, anger built inside him along with the pain, and the combined strain took its toll.

Ahmad and Zar had had marital problems before, but now they seemed to bring out the worst in each other, and by doing so, created a huge chasm of hate. The chasm grew larger and deeper, until neither one could find a way to bridge it.

By the time Ahmad's injury finally healed, his marriage was deathly ill. In the middle of this, an old friend from Afghanistan arrived to spend some time with them. Timur, who now made his home in Texas, had come to Salt Lake on an extended business trip. Ahmad hadn't seen Tim since their days in high school and did his best to put on a cheerful front.

It didn't take long for Tim to realize how depressed his friend was, and one evening, thinking it would cheer him up, Tim took Ahmad to a nightclub. Before entering, Tim offered Ahmad a few words of caution and advice.

"If you really want to talk to people in this country and be accepted by them, don't tell them your real name or where you're from. Americans think everyone from that part of the world is a terrorist or some kind of radical."

Ahmad could see the logic in this, but had no idea where that one night would lead. At the time, he only knew it felt good to be in a place where there was music, food and lots of people who were laughing and enjoying life.

Ahmad continued to visit night clubs after Tim returned to Texas, never giving people his real name or where he was from. The advice seemed to work, because in the weeks which followed, Ahmad made many friends, most of them women. Some of those friendships went even further. Afterwards, he felt guilty and full of remorse, but he tried to block those feelings, the same way he blocked the pain and the nightmares.

One night, Ahmad noticed a beautiful young woman sitting at one of the tables. Slim, sophisticated and attractive, she possessed many of the qualities he admired in a woman. Ahmad watched her for a long while before gathering enough nerve to approach her table. She glanced up and smiled at him, and moments later, they were caught up in conversation.

When Ahmad learned that Kathy was currently seeing another man, he didn't pursue the relationship. Then a year later, Ahmad saw that smile again.

Talking to Kathy, Ahmad found he could no longer pretend to be someone other than himself. There was something about those green eyes that demanded the truth. They deserved the truth.

As they talked, everything spilled out ... the months in Sedarat ...the torture and the nightmares ... even the problems with his marriage.

Kathy listened. Kathy understood. Kathy loved him. The spark of those simple, yet magical words ignited the flames of passion in him that had lain dormant since Angelique's last letter. Months passed and Ahmad discovered that in Kathy's arms the pain did more than just go away. It was almost as if it had never existed.

But admitting they were in love with each other brought its own kind of pain and problems.

Finally, Ahmad confessed everything to Zarghuna.

A month later, Ahmad was served with divorce papers while he was at work. Reality came crashing in and with it the horrible fear of losing his children. For a time, Ahmad and Zarghuna made an attempt at reconciliation, but eventually, they realized how useless and pathetic it was to be locked in a relationship they both hated.

Zarghuna hired an attorney and took Ahmad to court. To her surprise, he agreed to every term that she asked for. Ahmad rented a cheap apartment and moved out, leaving everything to his wife and children. He had no money, but the thing he wanted most was granted to him. Zarghuna agreed to let Ahmad have the boys every other weekend.

With time, the bitterness and hurt began to fade. Zar started taking English classes, got her driver's license, and found a job -- things she had been reluctant to do during the years of their marriage.

When it was all over, Kathy suggested that she and Ahmad fly to Germany to visit his sister Shaima, whom he hadn't seen in nine years.

The first four days of the trip were everything Ahmad had hoped for. He and Kathy and Shaima and Nazir visited many beautiful sites, picnicked in the park, laughed, talked and enjoyed Shaima's wonderful Afghan cooking.

Around eleven a.m., on the fifth day, Ahmad was sitting in the living room looking through some family photo albums, when the phone rang. Shaima and Kathy were in the kitchen, so Ahmad picked up the receiver. He was surprised and delighted to hear his sister Rahella's voice, calling from Pakistan.

Rahella was surprised as well, as she had expected Shaima to answer. In spite of her warm greeting, Ahmad sensed a kind of sadness in the way she talked. When he asked what was wrong, Rahella started to cry.

"This past year has been the worst year in the history of our family. I didn't want to bother anyone with it, but I have to talk to somebody who understands how I feel .... "

Ahmad listened in shocked silence as the grim facts spilled out between her sobs.

Mina and her husband had been killed by Communists ... Iqbal and Nazir's brother were murdered at the same time, but no one learned of their deaths until nearly six months later. Two cousins and an uncle had been killed in the war ...

Tragically, when the news about Mina and Farid finally surfaced, their mother had just been hospitalized after being hit by a sniper's bullet while riding a bus. Knowing what the news of her daughter's death would do to her, the family tried to keep things quiet. A nurse in the hospital unwittingly told Alima what had happened, not realizing the people involved were the woman's family. Alima died a few hours later ....

Ahmad's hands were shaking so hard he dropped the receiver. "Oh, God no .... Oh, God, no!" was all he could say.

Returning to Utah, Ahmad tried to go on with the every day demands of his life. Somehow, God would help him through the pain and grief. He had his job, his sons, and Kathy.

Then, barely one year later, Ahmad received word that his youngest brother, nineteen-year-old Rahim had been shot and killed. On top of so much tragedy and loss, this latest trauma proved too great for Hafiz, who suffered a nervous breakdown and was admitted to a mental hospital.

In the midst of his grief, Ahmad was determined to do something to protect the lives of those family members who remained. "I cannot bring back the ones that are gone," he told Kathy. "But the ones who are alive and need my help -- I will do anything, knock on any door, if there is even the smallest crack of hope to help them."

After months of extensive paperwork and meetings with people from the office of Senator Orrin Hatch, Ahmad received word that his sister Rahella, her husband and their children had received permission to enter the country and would arrive in Salt Lake City in seven days time.

Driving to the airport to meet them on the appointed day, Ahmad felt the waves of impatience and anticipation crashing on the shores of his heart and mind. It wasn't only Rahella, his little sister who was coming -- with her, she was bringing all the memories of his childhood, his country, and the loved ones he had left behind.

Rahella was like the rain in the springtime, washing away the dusty layers of time and distance from fragile memories of his former life.

Tears were welling in Ahmad's dark eyes even before the gate opened. Suddenly, there she was, making her way through the crowd with tears in her eyes and a big smile on her beautiful face.

Rahella's presence in the United States impressed upon Ahmad that the death of loved ones makes the bonds of loving and caring between surviving family members even stronger. In strengthening the bond between brother and sister, Ahmad began to feel a deeper, spiritual closeness to family members that were no longer with him. His father. Mina. And the loving presence of his mother ....

The day finally came when Ahmad was teasing Rahella about something and suddenly found himself smiling, remembering how much he enjoy teasing his mother.

Whenever he came home after school, Ahmad's mother was in the habit of asking him how he was and what his day was like. Hoping to confuse her, Ahmad would give his answer in French. Yet somehow, his mother seemed to understand what he said.

One day, as he was leaving for classes at the university, Ahmad confronted her with this. "You don't speak a word of French. How can you understand what I'm saying?"

His mother smiled and answered, "You're part of me. I carried you and felt your emotions and your heartbeat for nine months inside my being. I have been looking into your eyes since you were a baby. They are the windows of your emotions, and the tongue of your heart and thoughts. No matter how old you are, you will still be my little baby boy, and there is nothing -- not language, not distance, not even time, that could stop me from understanding you."

Remembering those words, Ahmad felt in his heart that if the love of a mother was that powerful, death would not stop her from watching over him. Nor would it stop him from feeling the presence of her soul in times of need.

Oh, my dearest mother! I miss you very much. I wish I could turn the clock backward so I could erase all the pain and the heartache that I caused you. I wish I could hear once again those beautiful lullabyes that made the angels accompany you from the heavens. How I long to contemplate your sleepless eyes watching the rain from the window, while you caressed my hair with your soothing, magical fingers. What I would give to be in your divine arms once more, protected by the gods of love, while the whole world was asleep.

Now I understand why they say that 'paradise is found beneath the feet of your mother'....

* * *

With Rahella and her family safely in Salt Lake, Ahmad began to work on getting Shaima and Nazir and their family permission to enter the United States. Negotiations moved slowly, but in a positive direction. In the meantime, his two boys were growing up in a free country with opportunities for education and an healthy appreciation of both cultures -- American and Afghan.

For a time, Ahmad felt as if heartache and loss were behind him. But as long as life exists, that will never be the case.

In spite of his love for her, Ahmad had to admit that his relationship with Kathy was slowly changing. Kathy had been a successful, goal-oriented, working woman when he met her, but he refused to believe that would get in the way of their love. Even the differences in their culture and religions hadn't mattered in the beginning. Instead, it seemed to enhance and add even more excitement to their romance.

Ahmad had thought that nothing could weaken their relationship, or change the love they felt for one another. But even love cannot exist without changing -- it either grows, or dies.

When Kathy told him that she wanted to quit her job in Utah and move back to Oregon where she had a brother and two sisters, Ahmad couldn't believe it. At first, he tried to discourage her from leaving, but that only created more conflict between them.

Finally, he gave in and told her that if moving away was what she really wanted, she ought to follow her heart.

The day before Kathy left for Oregon, she told Ahmad confidently, "I know that you love me enough to follow me anywhere in the world."

"The reasons that are taking you away from me, are the same reasons that are keeping me here in Salt Lake," Ahmad told her sadly. "My family."

During their first few weeks apart, Ahmad and Kathy wrote to each other and talked on the phone three or four times a month. Then, just as it had with Angelique so many years before, the distance between those letters and calls grew farther and farther apart.

One weekend, about a year and a half after Kathy moved to Oregon, Ahmad called to see how she was doing. Her mother answered the phone and told him, not realizing who was calling: "I'm sorry. Kathy won't be back until next week. She's on her honeymoon."

Kathy ... married. In spite of the time that had passed, the news coming so suddenly, was like a physical blow. How could she forget him so quickly?

Ahmad buried himself in his work, with family responsibilities, and sometimes, even in alcohol, trying to forget. But the loneliness, along with the unanswered questions remained.

At night, Ahmad would look up at the sky, and wonder what purpose he could have in life? He had faced the pain of death, but this kind of loss was brutally new to him.

During those silent times of despair, other memories and voices from that long ago 'square sky' returned with haunting urgency. Whenever he noticed a falling star, it was as if he could hear whispers in the night calling out to him. And when he slept, forgotten faces returned in his dreams, suddenly clear and familiar.

Ahmad felt as if those voices and faces were asking him to become a bridge of memory between the enlightened world where they had gone, and those left behind. And as he crossed this bridge, Ahmad thought more and more about the promise he and the other inmates had made to one another -- that whoever survived *Sedarat* should someday write the truth of what had happened there.

Like Ghezal, facing the task of a barn full of wheat, Ahmad didn't know where to begin, or how this miracle would be accomplished, but God willing, he would find a way.

Maybe now was the time to tell the story of that 'square sky.'

Perhaps this wasn't the end at all, but only a new beginning ....

chapter 25

The darkness in the cage, and the goodness in my
  heart have brightened my imagination so
  much
That I am finally able to see all the beauties
  of the garden of life.
Now the vision of freedom is not any less real than
  freedom itself.

ONE OF THE best books of knowledge is time. And some of the best lessons of our lives can be found in the pages of our memories. I believe there are crucial moments and experiences in each of our lives, when the veil of ignorance and obscurity shrinks from the shining face of truth. Between this veil and the light of truth are many shadows. Those shadows represent the difficulties, trials and pains which are a part of life. To me, the shadows in our lives are not negative unless we refuse to learn from them. When we do, they become shadows of understanding.

One of my life's most crucial moments began while I was in prison just before and shortly after the Russian invasion of my country. Until that time, the foundation of my hopes and dreams was based on the shaky ground of becoming someone important and making my life as comfortable as possible. But God had other plans for me.

During those months in prison, I shared the same cell with men from all walks of life, each of us living under inhuman conditions. Many of those inmates have vanished into the abyss of time, but each one left me with an important message -- whether for their loved ones or to the world.

There was the message of love from a young father to the baby he would never see because the arms of death were much closer to him than the tiny hands of his firstborn child. God knows how many times he looked through that window, searching for the stars that would help him shape the profile of his unborn innocent.

Then there was the message of a grandfather, who tried to relive the pleasant moments from his past by telling us some of the wonderful fairy tales he once shared with his grandchildren.

I will never forget the message of patriotism left by a silver-haired colonel who met death with a quiet smile. Or the message of miraculous power found in the words of an old man under torture -- "Allah toba ... God forgive me."

And always, I will carry with me the message of that single, blood-red tear on my hand.

My experiences under the "square sky" have given me a deeper connection with all human beings, regardless of their race, religion, culture, nationality, or any of the other differences that separate us from one another. This connection even defies the distance of time and space.

For example, the tragic loss of my own family members has enabled me to feel the sorrow of Jewish children who witnessed their loved ones burned to ashes in the concentration camps. And the echoes of all those tortured voices within the walls of *Sedarat*, have given my ears the sensitivity to hear the cries of mothers who have had husbands and children die in Bosnia, Ireland, Afghanistan and other countries throughout the world.

The fading eyes of an unknown man in my arms, and the stain of his single tear on my hand, has opened my heart to the grieving hearts of parents in Ethiopia, Samalia and Rwanda, when they looked into the helpless eyes of their starving children.

And the strength of my beliefs since childhood, when I sat cross-legged on the floor reading passages from the Holy Koran, has helped me respect and admire the love and innocence of a Christian boy when he kneels down and prays to the same God who is Father to us all.

It makes no difference whether these people lived centuries before me, or thousands of miles away. I know them and understand their pain. We share a bond that won't be affected by time or space, religion or race.

Each one of us has been blessed with the ability to learn from our experiences, both good and bad, as well as the experiences of others, if we so choose. Like the "square sky" in our prison room, we each have a window inside through which we can see the reflection of our deepest thoughts. If we would only share the visions from these windows with one another ... learning, loving, and helping each another along the way ... life could be a peaceful haven of dreams.

There is far greater power to be found in the blossoms of love and forgiveness than the strength of those who rule nations and possess all the weapons of war. I witnessed that power every time I saw the weak arms of prisoners binding each other's wounds and lifting those who had fallen; I heard it burning in their prayers and in the trembling words of an old man ... and I felt it in the touch of that single tear.

Now, after fifteen years, the power and meaning of these visions and messages shines clearer than ever. God is not the author of pain and suffering. He loves and cares for all His children, and wisely allows us to experience the tears, as well as the smiles of this life.

The powerful current of all those smiles and tears seems to meet and flow together whenever I recall that cold winter night -- the night I stood on a riverbank and saw the shimmering faces of my own losses and heard the echoes of my own tears carried by the whispers of the *Hari Rode* -- the angel that was crying like a river.

The End